SPEAKING ILL OF THE DEAD:

Jerks in Arizona History

SPEAKING ILL OF THE DEAD:

Jerks in Arizona History

Sam Lowe

Guilford, Connecticut

To my fellow Arizonans, who have lived long and prospered
despite some rather shaky ancestry.

To buy books in quantity for corporate use
or incentives, call **(800) 962-0973**
or e-mail **premiums@GlobePequot.com.**

Copyright © 2012 by Morris Book Publishing, LLC

Text design by Sheryl P. Kober
Project editor: Meredith Dias
Layout artist: Milly Iacono

Library of Congress Cataloging-in-Publication Data

Lowe, Sam.
  Speaking ill of the dead : jerks in Arizona history / Sam Lowe.
    p. cm.
  Includes bibliographical references and index.
  ISBN 978-0-7627-2815-2
  1. Arizona—History—Anecdotes. 2. Arizona—Biography—Anecdotes. 3.
Outlaws—Arizona—Biography—Anecdotes. 4. Rogues and
vagabonds—Arizona—Biography—Anecdotes. 5.
Criminals—Arizona—Biography—Anecdotes. I. Title. II. Title: Jerks in
Arizona history.
  F811.6.L685 2012
  979.1—dc23

                            2011048048

Printed in the United States of America

10 9 8 7 6 5 4 3 2 1

Contents

Acknowledgments

My sincere gratitude to Marshall Trimble, for his help in acquiring photographs of scurrilous characters; to George Berg, for enhancing many of the photographs; to Lyn, my wife, for teaching me how to move the photos from file to file; to Marilee Lasch and Bob Boze Bell, for their sketches of camera-shy outlaws; and to Tina Clark, Nancy Cannon, Chet Sagaser, and the kind people at the Arizona State Archives for helping with the research.

Introduction

Not all of Arizona's bad people lived out their lives in the years long-gone. However, there is a tendency to judge the state from the perspective of the scars left by those who gave it a bad name during its formative years. The following pages will give brief accounts of why those people are historically important, even though their impact wasn't always beneficial to the state.

They were robbers and killers, con men and rustlers, lawmen who went bad, and thieves. Few had any redeeming qualities. Despite that, they are a part of Arizona history and their stories are worth repeating.

So here are a few of them, presented as factually as possible, considering that none of them wrote down much of anything relating to their personal lives. The following tales, therefore, are comprehensive reports, based on the truths and the fiction that regularly accompany such storytelling attempts.

Sam Lowe
September 2011

CHAPTER ONE
Jacob Waltz:
An Inadvertent Cause of Death

In the strictest sense of the word, Jacob Waltz may not have been a killer. But in a roundabout way, he was responsible for a number of documented fatalities. It all depends on how well fact holds up against legend. The trouble is, there is no clear line of definition between the two.

According to reliable records, Jacob Waltz was a German immigrant who prospected and farmed in the mountains and flatlands of Arizona. He was born near Oberschwandorf, Baden-Württemberg, Germany, around 1810. He came to the United States in 1839. He arrived in Arizona Territory in 1863 and moved to the Phoenix area in 1868. He died on October 25, 1891. He is buried in Phoenix.

Almost everything else about Jacob Waltz is legend, supposition, guesswork, and despite exhaustive research, little more than speculation—especially the parts about how he acquired the gold mine now known as the Lost Dutchman Mine, and whatever happened to the treasure that supposedly lies in it.

Some historians say he became the owner of the fabulously wealthy digs either by murdering his partner or by killing a group of Mexican miners. Others say he came by it legitimately, purchasing it from a family of miners. And some say there never was a mine, but that it existed only in the mind of an aged prospector.

The debate continues.

So does the search.

Although he was German, Waltz was known as "the Dutchman" by the time he arrived in Arizona. The nickname apparently was a derivation of "the Deutschman," altered because it was easier to say. Historians also believe he changed his last name from Walz to Waltz to better match its pronunciation. After arriving

Weaver's Needle is a focal point for those seeking Jacob Waltz's Lost Dutchman gold mine.
SAM LOWE PHOTO

in the United States, he spent twenty years prospecting across the Midwest and Southwest. In 1863, he staked his first claim in the Bradshaw Mountains near Prescott. A short time later, he signed a petition urging Governor John Goodwin to provide area miners with military protection against Indian raids. According to records, he filed several other claims, but apparently none of them paid big rewards.

In 1870, he took a job at the Vulture Mine in Wickenburg where he supposedly met Jacob Weiser. (Some writers believe Weiser was Waltz's nephew and that they migrated together.) There is also an inference that during his time in Wickenburg, Waltz became involved with an Apache woman who helped him steal ore from the mine in a practice known as "high grading." That, according to the story, was the source of his gold, not the mine in the Superstition Mountains as many came to believe later on.

Waltz and Weiser formed a loose partnership and decided to look for a fabulous treasure they had heard about, hidden deep in the Superstitions east of Phoenix. From that point on, the story of Jacob Waltz and the Lost Dutchman Mine becomes a mixture of fact and fiction, blended with deception, accusations, and speculation.

According to one theory, the two miners saved a Mexican man's life and he repaid them by giving them a map that showed the location of the mine. The man was Miguel Peralta, son of Gonzales Peralta and grandson of Don Miguel Peralta, who had discovered the mine years before and took a substantial amount of gold from it before most of his workmen were massacred by the Apaches who considered the area sacred. According to their ancient beliefs, the gold had been placed there by the Thunder God of the Mountain and must never fall into the hands of anyone besides the Apaches. Waltz and Weiser not only found the mine, so the story goes, but eventually bought it from the remaining members of the Peralta family.

Other stories suggest that the two stumbled upon the mine by accident. Or that they killed two Mexican miners, stole their gold, and told others it had come from the mine, which was in "such rough country that you could be right in the mine without seeing it." He also claimed that the ore was in a vein as much as eighteen inches thick, and that it was easily retrieved. Regardless of how they got their hands on the gold, the two soon became big spenders in the Phoenix area for several years, until Weiser mysteriously disappeared. Again, there were rumors and questions. Some figured Waltz had grown tired of sharing the wealth so he disposed of his partner in a dispute over ownership.

A more likely story is that Weiser stayed at the mine while Waltz returned to Phoenix to buy supplies. When Waltz returned after five days, he found their camp destroyed and their animals missing. He also found Weiser's body, spread-eagled across a fire. The scene scared Waltz so badly that he fled back into town, raving about an Apache attack. When he regained some sense of composure, Waltz went back to the site and buried his partner. He said it was the last time he went back to the site. He claimed that he hid the mine opening, and then covered the trail leading to it by tying blankets to the back of his mule to sweep away tracks.

Despite his tales of rich ore, Waltz never filed a claim for the mine. Also, he refused to talk about Weiser's death after giving his initial account. Years later, when his version of what happened was met with derision and snickers of disbelief, Waltz responded that anyone looking for his gold should find Weiser's grave because he buried him near the mine. And, despite telling others that he never returned to the mine, Waltz did make frequent trips into the Superstitions and usually came back with more gold nuggets. Not a huge amount, but enough to sustain him until his next junket.

Meanwhile, the stories abounded. Those who didn't believe he had actually found the old Peralta mine figured he probably held up stagecoaches to get his spending money. And some insisted he had stumbled across a cache hidden by the Spaniards before they were killed by the Apaches. When would-be fortune hunters asked him to reveal the location, he gave conflicting directions. Some tried to follow him into the mountains, but he easily eluded them. And many of those who tried to follow him never came back.

About the only constant in all the stories is that the mine was (or is) located somewhere near Weaver's Needle, a towering lava plug that has become a symbol of the Superstitions. Don Peralta had named it Sombrero Peak; others dubbed it "the Finger of God." The current name comes from Paulino Weaver, an early explorer who carved his name into the base. Subsequent treasure hunters saw his name and applied it to the landmark.

Regardless of how he got the gold, Waltz became well-known in the Phoenix area, frequently buying drinks and paying for them with nuggets. But time ran out before he was able to spend all his money.

Several months after his last excursion into the mountains, Waltz came down with pneumonia. He lived alone in a simple adobe house near the Salt River on the outskirts of Phoenix, raised a few chickens and kept to himself except when he ventured into a local saloon. In February 1891, a monstrous flood swept across the Phoenix area, commonly known as the Valley of the Sun. The rushing waters demolished the small house; Waltz saved himself by climbing up a mesquite tree and tying himself to the branches. He was stranded there for almost two days before being rescued.

Not surprisingly, there are conflicting details about the rescue.

In one version, he was saved by Johnny Griejalva and his son, Juan, who cut him loose, took him to their home, then to the home of Julia Thomas. In another, his saviors were Herman and Reinhardt Petrasch, who rode their horses through the flooded landscape to check on the old hermit. They said they found Waltz sitting in his house; he told them he had lashed himself to the tree, but got down when the waters receded. Either way, he had pneumonia and it was bad.

So bad that Julia Thomas couldn't save him.

Waltz had befriended Thomas when she came to his place to buy eggs. He offered to give her money after learning that she was in debt and in danger of losing her business, an ice cream parlor. Up until that time, she thought he was just a poor old farmer who wore tattered clothing. She quickly changed her mind when Waltz showed her gold ore worth more than one thousand dollars.

The Dutchman spent the entire summer in his sickbed in Thomas's home. He told her and Reinhardt Petrasch that he wanted them to go to his former home and retrieve something. Most of the adobe house was gone, washed away by the worst flood ever to sweep across the territory. But they were able to recover five sacks of gold nuggets, which they placed in a box under his bed. Too sick to spend them himself, Waltz gave the nuggets to Thomas to help pay off the mortgage on her store, and to reward her for taking care of him.

As he grew weak and feverish, the Dutchman promised to tell Thomas and Dick Holmes, another old prospector, how to find the mine. But by that time, his condition was so bad that he could merely utter short sentences and unintelligible words. He managed to tell them that the mine was in the northwest corner of the Superstitions and that they were to look for a stripped palo verde tree. He also said he had left several clues about the location, but they were sketchy.

He died on October 25, 1891, without leaving a map or giving exact directions to his lost mine. Although she wasn't sure about where to look, Julia Thomas mounted an expedition to go find it. She sold her business, invested every penny she had, and rode into the Superstitions, accompanied by Dick Holmes and the Petrasch brothers. The *Arizona Republican* reported it under the headline, "A Queer Quest in Search of Gold." The accompanying story reported that Thomas "is now in the Superstition Mountains engaged in a work usually deemed strange for a woman's sphere. She is prospecting for a lost mine . . ."

The group returned empty-handed and Thomas never made another attempt. Prior to her death on December 24, 1917, she eked out a meager living selling Lost Dutchman Mine maps for seven dollars each.

But her lack of success did not deter others.

Since 1870, when stories about the mine first started circulating, hundreds have set out to find it, and an estimated forty people have either disappeared or been found dead in and around the suspected location.

One of them was Guy "Hematite" Frank, who returned from the mountains in 1937 with a large amount of rich gold samples. After he went back for more, he was found shot to death on the side of a trail. Next to his body was a small sack of gold ore.

Author Barry Storm claimed he narrowly escaped death when a sniper took a shot at him as he did research for his book, *Thunder God's Gold,* in 1945. Storm speculated that the unknown gunman might have also been responsible for the earlier death of one Adolph Ruth.

In 1947, prospector James Carvey employed a helicopter to search for the mine. The pilot set him down near Weaver's Needle, but Carvey failed to hike out according to his plan. A search crew found his camp but not Carvey. Months later, a headless skeleton was discovered in a canyon and identified as his.

Engineer Robert St. Marie attempted to find the lost gold by drilling a hole through Weaver's Needle in 1960. He was shot and killed by Edward Piper, a prospector, during a claims dispute. While awaiting trial, Piper was found dead, allegedly of a perforated ulcer.

In 1984, the body of prospector Wade Gasler was found near the alleged mine site. He had spent much of his adult life searching for the treasure. In his backpack, authorities discovered gold that, when assayed, had the same characteristics as the rich ore Jacob Waltz had produced years earlier.

A Colorado prospector, Jesse Capen, went missing in the area in December 2009. His campsite was found abandoned, but he was never located. Capen had expressed interest in the mine for several years and had made previous trips to where he thought it might be.

On July 11, 2010, three hikers from Utah went missing in the Superstitions while looking for the mine. They were identified as Curtis Merworth, age forty-nine, Ardean Charles, sixty-six, and Malcolm Meeks, forty-one. Merworth had been lost in the same area a year before, and had to be rescued. Rescue crews headed by the Maricopa County Sheriff's Office, spent more than a week looking for the men, but the search was called off on July 19. Their remains were recovered in January 2011. The assumption was that they died from exposure to the blistering summer heat.

Many have tried; none have succeeded. There are, however, other ways of mining the Lost Dutchman Mine for monetary reward. For example, the creation and sale of Lost Dutchman maps has become a cottage industry. They're sold in gift shops, mining equipment stores, and tourist information centers all across Arizona. The mine has become the subject of numerous books, and was featured in the movie *Lust for Gold,* filmed in 1949 and starring Glenn Ford and Ida Lupino.

But those who seek hidden treasure need not despair. If they can't find the Dutchman's Mine, there are plenty of other opportunities within Arizona's borders because there's lost gold all over the state.

The problem, however, remains the same:

Where is it?

Jacob Waltz was buried in a pioneer and military cemetery in Phoenix.
SAM LOWE PHOTO

For starters, some members of the Tohono O'odham tribe of southeastern Arizona believe that their sacred Baboquivera Mountain Range is filled with gold. They claim all the gold ever found in the state filtered down from there and there's plenty left. According to their traditions, I'Itoi, the god who created them, lives in a cave on the mountain and sometimes comes down to give the people advice. Many years ago, they say, Spanish explorers were digging for the gold when the mountain opened up and swallowed them.

Other caches aren't guarded by the gods, but they're just as hard to find.

Up near Lake Powell, the stories about John D. Lee's hidden treasure are still told around the campfires. Lee was a Mormon settler who participated in the slaughter of 122 pioneers in Utah's 1857 Mountain Meadows Massacre. Before he was arrested, prosecuted, convicted, and executed by the church's leaders, Lee fled the Mormon compound and hid in one of the many canyons that slice across the Arizona-Utah border. According to a letter he wrote to one of his nineteen wives, Lee hid his life savings in the canyon and sent her a map showing the location.

Some of the stories say his buried treasure included seven cans filled with pure gold; others say it was gold coins worth more than one hundred thousand dollars, stolen from the settlers he had helped murder. It's probable that Lee did hide some treasure somewhere in the canyons, but he hid it so well that nobody ever found it.

Another fortune lies buried, in the literal sense, at Sunset Crossing on the Little Colorado River. In 1865, the story is told, a prospector who had struck it rich in California's gold field was returning to his home in Illinois, accompanied by his now-wealthy wife. He allegedly was carrying a bonanza of about three hundred thousand dollars in gold dust when they arrived at the crossing. But his wife fell ill and died within a matter of days.

A sympathetic trading post owner built a wooden coffin and cleared some land for a gravesite, and as the hastily arranged funeral procession walked to the burial site, the pall bearers noted that the casket was particularly heavy. No one thought much about it at the time, and the prospector left. Many years later, according to this legend, he told friends that he had placed half his fortune, an estimated one hundred fifty thousand dollars, in the coffin alongside his wife's body. The revelation produced a flurry of activity, but no one ever found the grave, the coffin, or the gold.

Another intriguing story of lost treasure involves missionaries and Indians. In it, Spanish friars founded Tumacacori, a mission near present-day Tubac. Shortly after moving in, they also discovered a rich silver mine and forced the Opata Indians to work it for them. After the ore was smelted, the bars of silver were stacked in a large area inside the mine. The laborers also used the room for their own religious practices, a combination of the missionaries' teachings and their own paganism. During one rite, they were led to believe that one of their people, a young maiden, was actually the Blessed Virgin Mary. They ordered her to mate with their chief to produce a child savior. When she refused, her captors sacrificed her to appease their gods. They bound her and placed her on the stack of silver bars, gave her one final chance to accept their demands, then murdered her and went into a frenzied ritual dance.

When the missionaries heard the commotion, they rushed to the mine and found the young woman's body. Aghast that their teachings had produced such a dreadful result, the holy men drove the Indians away then sealed the mine entrance. The legend says that the silver bars and the woman's skeleton still lie beneath the ground near the mission, waiting to be found. Retrieving the treasure is now impossible because the mission and surrounding area are now Tumacacori National Monument and the federal government doesn't allow digging.

The same two principal groups were also involved in another tale of lost gold. In this one, the ancestors of the current Tohono O'odham tribe helped the missionaries build a church and a peaceful little village surrounding it north of the Arizona-Mexico border. The holy men named it San Marcelo de Sonoita, and then ordered the natives to work a gold mine in the San Francisco Mountains to the south, across the Mexican border.

They also built a smelter and converted the refined gold dust into bars, which were stored, along with bags of precious dust, in a large vault under the floor of the mission. The gold was supposed to be shipped back to Spain but it never got there. According to the legend, the natives grew tired of being overworked and rebelled one Sunday in 1750. A group of tribe members walked into the morning service at the mission with blankets thrown over their upper bodies, as was their custom. When they filled the church, the men pulled out weapons from beneath the blankets and killed three missionaries. Then they threw the bodies into the underground chamber and destroyed the church, leaving only the foundations. They also covered the entrance to the gold mine where they had been subjected to years of forced labor. No trace of either the mission or the mine has ever been found.

However, another version of that tale says the Indians were actually loyal to the friars. When they heard of plans for an attack by a neighboring tribe, they helped the priests hide the gold in a cave in the Tortilla Mountains, and then led them to safety. Nobody ever found the cave. Or the gold.

Whispers of another legendary treasure still drift over the desert flatlands around Gila Bend. The story tells about three soldiers who were sent out to rescue a rancher's daughter who had been kidnapped by Apache raiders. They didn't find the abducted girl, but they did stumble across a waterhole filled with nuggets of pure gold. Directly above, they also found two gold-bearing veins, one five inches across, the other sixteen inches wide.

The troopers filled their saddlebags and headed back toward Fort Grant. But they ran out of water and had to separate. One died on the parched desert floor. The second staggered back to the fort on foot. He had to abandon his horse and was so crazed by the heat and lack of water that no one ever believed his story. The third soldier did arrive back safely and became a rich man. After his discharge from the Army, he led several expeditions back to the site but was never able to relocate it. In 1881, his body was found in the desert of Yuma County. He was on foot but carrying his saddlebags. The saddlebags were filled with gold nuggets. Or so the story goes.

But the lure of the Lost Dutchman Mine still commands the most attention.

After Julia Thomas and her associates failed to find the gold, interest waned for several years, primarily because most considered Waltz a mentally disturbed old man who spun fanciful stories about lost treasure and Indian attacks. The subject didn't get much attention in 1916, when two miners found an old Spanish saddle bag filled with sixteen thousand dollars' worth of smelted gold near the site of the Peralta massacre. Although the discovery gave some credibility to the stories repeated so often by Waltz, it did not send thousands into the hills looking for the rest of the treasure.

But it became an item of national interest in the summer of 1931, when amateur explorer and treasure hunter Adolph Ruth disappeared while searching for the mine. His skull was found six months later. It had two bullet holes in it, and the story made national headlines, which sparked a renewed interest in the mine.

Ruth claimed to have knowledge of the mine because his son, Erwin, once gave a man some legal aid that helped him avoid prison time. In gratitude, the almost-inmate told the younger Ruth about the storied Peralta mine and gave him some aged maps. Although he was sixty-six years old at the time, Adolph Ruth decided to go after the treasure. He ignored the advice of friends who told him that the treacherous mountains were no place for even a skilled outdoorsman, much less a man of his age. He did not return as scheduled. In December 1931, the *Arizona Republic* reported that a skull had been found and, after examination of dental records and several photographs, it was determined that it was Ruth's.

The rest of his body was discovered a short distance away, along with many of Ruth's personal effects. Among them were a fully loaded pistol and his checkbook, which contained a note in Ruth's handwriting that claimed he had found the mine and gave detailed directions. His final words on the note were "veni, vidi, vici." Neither the alleged map nor the alleged mine were ever found.

The story was front-page news in publications growing weary of reporting on the Great Depression. That was impetus enough for those who seek wealth by digging holes in the ground, and the searches resumed in earnest. But, as far as anyone knows, they have all been in vain.

Jacob Waltz was buried in the southwest corner of a pioneer and military cemetery in downtown Phoenix. His grave is marked by a replica of a mine entrance.

In 1977, twelve acres adjacent to the Tonto National Forest, which contains the Superstition Mountains, were set aside as the Lost Dutchman State Park. Easily accessible, it is now a favorite destination for hikers and campers who commune with nature amidst the brush and cactus. Strategically placed signs give the natural history of the area and warn about rattlesnakes. Other signs caution that serious gold prospecting is not allowed.

CHAPTER TWO

Johnny Ringo:
The Bad-Tempered Bad Man

Like many of his contemporaries, Johnny Ringo lived a violent life and died a violent death. Unlike several of the others, however, there was an unmistakable finality about his demise. Nobody claimed he had cheated death; there were no rumors that he had been spotted in Texas or living on a ranch in Mexico. On July 14, 1882, Johnny Ringo was found dead and his story was over.

Well, not exactly.

Although he was most certainly dead, there was immediate speculation about who killed him. Several names arose, including Wyatt Earp and John "Doc" Holliday, who were being blamed for almost every gunshot death at the time, as well as gunslinger Frank Leslie and gambler Mike O'Rourke.

But the most likely suspect was Johnny Ringo.

According to those who discovered his body, Ringo used his own gun to end his life with a bullet to the head. A preponderance of the available evidence supported that contention. But others weren't so sure, and the debate over who pulled the trigger goes on more than 120 years later.

There were some irrefutable facts. The primary one was that Ringo's body was found leaning against a large tree in West Turkey Creek Canyon with a bullet hole in his right temple and an exit wound at the back of his head. His revolver was hanging from the finger of his right hand. One round had been fired. His feet were wrapped in pieces of his undershirt. The horse that carried him there was missing. It would be discovered later, about two miles away, and still wearing a saddle with the dead man's boots attached to it. The coroner ruled it suicide. Ringo was buried near the tree where he had taken his last breath.

Although Johnny Ringo committed suicide,
some believe he was killed by Wyatt Earp.
SCOTTSDALE CC SOUTHWEST STUDIES

(His grave is still located in West Turkey Creek Canyon, on private property that is part of the Coronado National Forest in Cochise County. Those who desire to see it must check in with the owners first.)

Apparently, not many felt really bad about the death of Johnny Ringo.

Two months before it happened, Tombstone historian George Parsons wrote in his diary:

Excitement again this morning. Sheriff [Johnny Behan] went out with a posse supposedly to arrest the Earp party, but they will never do it. The cowboy element is backing him [Behan] strongly. Johnny Ringo being one of the [cowboys]. There is a prospect of a bad time and there are about three men who deserve to get it in the back of the neck. Terrible thing, this, for our town, but the sooner it is all over with the better.

Behan was a Ringo ally and a key figure in Tombstone at the time. He had been appointed the first sheriff of Cochise County after it was created by dividing up Pima County. Prior to that, he had served as undersheriff of Pima County, which included Tombstone. When he was given the new assignment, Wyatt Earp succeeded him as undersheriff. The two never got along well, and the tension heightened when Behan's common-law wife, Josephine Sadie Marcus, left him and took up with Earp.

Behan's love life was also the subject of much local speculation. He and his first wife, Victoria, lived in Prescott where he served as Yavapai County sheriff and was twice elected to the Territorial Legislature. After Victoria divorced him for "consorting with prostitutes and other women of low moral character," he met Josephine; they moved to Tombstone, and lived together without benefit of a marriage license or ceremony. That relationship ended when Josephine arrived home from San Francisco unexpectedly and caught Behan in bed with one of her best friends.

The embarrassing situation got even worse when the *Tombstone Epitaph* found it worthy of a front-page story. Earp soon ended his common-law marriage with Mattie Blaylock and took up with Josephine Marcus. The two eventually married and stayed together until his death.

Shortly after he arrived in Tombstone, Behan took a job as a bartender at the Grand Hotel, a favorite hangout of a loosely knit band of outlaws who called themselves "the Cowboys." He befriended many of them and, after he became sheriff, was reluctant to arrest them for alleged crimes.

Behan was a witness to the infamous gunfight at the OK Corral. He tried to stop the fight but failed to convince either side to lay down their guns and settle the feud without bloodshed. Members of the Earp faction had no respect for him and were determined to put an end to the longstanding quarrel; the Clanton-led Cowboys had publicly threatened the Earps and Holliday so many times that they couldn't back down. So both sides ignored Behan's warning that if they persisted, there'd be violence.

They persisted.

There was violence.

When the well-documented shootout ended, three members of the Clanton gang were dead.

Behan arrested the Earps and Holliday and testified against them at a preliminary hearing, but the presiding judge ruled there wasn't enough evidence to indict anyone for murder. Behan stuck around Tombstone until 1887, when he moved to Yuma and became assistant superintendent of the Yuma Territorial Prison. He saved a guard's life and killed a prisoner during an escape attempt and, in April 1888, was promoted to prison superintendent. George Parsons, the Tombstone historian, would later comment that he thought Behan was "on the wrong side of the bars."

The ex-sheriff left Arizona and moved to Philadelphia, then Washington, D.C. His political connections landed him government positions in Texas, and then he fought in the Spanish-American War and the Boxer Rebellion. By 1901, he was back in Arizona, working for the *Tucson Citizen*. Two years later, he returned to Texas, where he unsuccessfully ran for sheriff of El Paso County.

Finally back in Arizona in 1910, he served as a railroad policeman and supervised a survey party along the Colorado River. He died in Tucson on June 7, 1912.

But Behan's association with Johnny Ringo was never mentioned when the *Tombstone Epitaph,* in a roundabout way, rose to Ringo's defense in its obituary notice:

> *[Ringo] was recognized by friends and foes as a recklessly brave man, who would go any distance, or undergo any hardship, to serve a friend or punish an enemy.*

Four days after the fatality, the *Arizona Daily Star*'s report didn't take sides, but spelled Ringo's name incorrectly:

> *John Ringgold, one of the best known men in southeastern Arizona, was found dead in Morse's canyon, in the Chiricahua Mountains last Friday. He evidently committed suicide. He was known in this section as "King of the Cowboys," and was fearless in the extreme. He had many staunch friends and bitter enemies. The pistol, with one chamber emptied, was found in his clenched fist. He shot himself in the head, the bullet entering the right side, between the eye and ear, and coming out on top of his head. Some members of the family reside in San Jose, California.*

The coroner's verdict of suicide was readily accepted by the townspeople. Ringo had been showing signs of depression. Tombstone's glory days were coming to an abrupt end. The silver mines were petering out and the miners were leaving, so the demand for beef was dwindling, which meant rustlers weren't making as much money as before. Since he was a regular practitioner of the illegal trade, Ringo could no longer rely on that income. After many of his friends had been killed or arrested, he started binge drinking, often staying drunk for days. He left Tombstone to visit his sisters in San Jose, but they rejected him due to his wild reputation.

Depressed, drunk, and lonely, Ringo returned to Tombstone, then rode off into the wilderness and set up camp at West Turkey Creek. He removed his boots and tied them to the saddle so scorpions wouldn't sneak inside. He picketed his horse but it got loose and wandered off, so he tore up his undershirt and tied the pieces around his feet to protect them while he went chasing after his mount. When he couldn't find the horse, he returned to his campsite and, despondent over the way things were going, shot himself.

He was thirty-two years old.

The coroner's report included sworn statements by the men who found the corpse. Part of it read:

The undersigned [John Yoast] viewed the body and found it in a sitting posture, facing west, the head inclined to the right. There was a bullet hole in the right temple, the bullet coming out the top of the left side . . . Several of the undersigned identify the body as that of John Ringo, well known in Tombstone. He was dressed in light hat, blue shirt, vest, pants and drawers, on his feet were a pair of hose and undershirt torn up so as to protect his feet. He had evidentially traveled but a short distance in this footgear. His revolver he grasps in his right hand, his rifle rested against the tree close to him . . .

Robert Boller, who was also there when the body was discovered, wrote many years later:

I showed him [Yoast] where the bullet had entered the tree on the left side. Blood and brains oozing from the wound and matted his hair. There was an empty shell in the six-shooter and the hammer was on that. I called it suicide fifty-two years ago, and I am still calling it suicide. I guess I'm the last of the coroner's jury.

Despite that, the rumors flew, several of which implicated Wyatt Earp as the killer. According to those theories, Earp was gunning for Ringo because he believed Ringo was involved in the shooting death of Wyatt's brother Morgan. The speculation was that Earp and his associates spotted Ringo sitting next to a campfire and Wyatt shot him with a rifle. Most of those allegations, however, were put forth by writers in the 1920s. One of them even quoted Josephine Earp, Wyatt's wife, as saying that her husband had told her he shot Ringo. But legitimate historians point out that Wyatt had left Tombstone more than three months earlier, moved to Denver and never returned to Arizona. He also denied the killing during an interview in Denver in 1896.

Doc Holliday also was suspected. The suspicion was that he had stepped in and killed Ringo to save his friend, Wyatt Earp, the trouble of doing it himself. But official records indicate he was in District Court in Pueblo County, Colorado, at the time, making it impossible to be in Arizona simultaneously. Some historians, however, refute that claim with allegations that only Holliday's attorney was in court, so there's an outside chance that Doc might have done Ringo in. But most still say it was unlikely.

Frank Leslie got himself involved when he claimed responsibility for Ringo's death while serving a term in Yuma Territorial Prison for murdering his wife. The convict told his story to a prison guard but it was ignored because Leslie was a known braggart who appeared to be trying to take credit for the shooting in the hope that it would increase his stature among his fellow inmates. Mike O'Rourke, the gambler, was considered because Ringo had welched on a gambling debt. Neither of those theories held up under closer examination, and the suicide verdict was generally accepted.

There wasn't much in Ringo's early life to indicate that he'd wind up dead in an Arizona canyon. He was born on May 3, 1850, in Greenfork, Indiana, the son of Martin and Mary Peters Ringo. The family moved to Missouri, then hooked up with a wagon train in Liberty and headed west to California in 1864. His mother kept a journal during the trek. One of the entries, written as they crossed Wyoming, declared:

And now oh God comes the saddest record of my life for this day my husband accidentally shot himself and was buried by the wayside and oh, my heart is breaking, if I had no children how gladly would I lay down with my dead . . .

An eyewitness account published in the *Liberty Tribune* back in Missouri gave the details:

Just after daylight on the morning of the 30th July Mr. Ringo stepped out . . . of the wagons as, I suppose, for the purpose of looking around to see if Indians were in sight and his shotgun went off accidentally in his own hands, the load entering the right eye and coming out at the top of his head. At the report of his gun I saw his hat blow up 20 feet in the air and his brains were scattered in all directions. To see the agony and distress of his wife and children was painful in the extreme . . .

Johnny and his three sisters witnessed the tragedy. He was fourteen. After their father was buried along the trail, the survivors resumed their journey to California. Five years later, Ringo was in Texas where he became involved in the Mason County Range War, more commonly known as the Hoodoo War. It pitted German immigrants who had been loyal to the Union during the Civil War against Confederate sympathizers.

The rivalry erupted in full-scale warfare when Elijah and Pete Backus, jailed on rustling charges, were dragged from their cells and lynched by a predominantly German mob. Ringo had sided with the rebel group and befriended Scott Cooley, a former Texas Ranger who was accused of several murders. When Cooley's father was killed by Peter Bader, a German farmer, he and Ringo launched a war of retribution against their rivals. Cooley retaliated by killing John Worley, a German deputy sheriff. He scalped the man and threw his body down a well. Another early victim of the fighting was Moses Baird, a Cooley supporter who was killed during an ambush allegedly staged by the German faction. On September 25, 1875, Ringo and another cowboy rode to the home of James Cheyney, the man they suspected of luring Baird into the ambush. Cheyney came out of his house unarmed and invited the two in for a meal. Both Ringo and his companion emptied their six-guns at Cheyney and left his body on the porch.

Later, Cooley and Ringo teamed up to shoot and kill Charley Bader after they mistook him for his brother Peter, the man who had killed Cooley's father. Both were arrested and jailed in Burnet, Texas. However, friends broke them out of jail and they parted company to evade further dealings with Texas lawmen.

The Mason County War unofficially ended in November 1876. More than a dozen men had been killed and Scott Cooley was also believed dead. Ringo was back in jail on an unknown charge and shared a cell with John Wesley Hardin, a notorious killer who gunned people down just for sport. Hardin complained that he didn't like being jailed with someone as vicious as Ringo. Although there is nothing documented about the disposal of the case, Ringo apparently was acquitted. He stayed in Texas for a couple more years and, at one point, served as a constable in Loyal Valley.

Then he moved to Arizona, winding up in Tombstone in 1879. It didn't take long before he allied himself with the band of outlaws known as the Cowboys and began his career as a rustler.

Although stories about Ringo didn't reach legendary proportions, he had already established a bad reputation due to his vile temper, especially when he was drinking. He shot Louis Hancock in a bar when Hancock refused his offer to buy him a shot of whiskey, saying he preferred beer. Although wounded in the throat, Hancock survived. Two years later, Ringo lost heavily in a poker game. He left the bar, then returned and robbed the other players of $500. When he sobered up, he returned the money but was arrested anyway.

Shortly after the Earps and Clantons shot it out, Ringo got drunk, accosted Doc Holliday on a Tombstone street, and challenged him to a shootout. Ringo claimed Holliday and Wyatt

Earp had wrongly accused him of robbing a stagecoach. The confrontation ended without a shot being fired when James Flynn, the new chief of police, put a choke hold on Ringo from behind. Both he and Holliday were hauled into court and fined for carrying weapons in town.

Two months later, Morgan Earp was murdered while playing pool in a Tombstone saloon. Because of his relationship with the Cowboys, and because the Cowboys were the primary suspects, Ringo was considered guilty by association, but no charges were ever filed. Sheriff Behan deputized Ringo to ride with the posse organized to go after Wyatt Earp when he went on his revenge-minded killing spree across Arizona, but nobody was ever taken. Within months, most of Ringo's friends were either dead or forced out of the territory.

Ringo then made the trip back home to San Jose, where his sisters not only rejected him, but even tried to hide the fact that he was their brother. Dejected, he returned to Tombstone and his eventual death.

But the name carries on.

The legend of Johnny Ringo has become a staple in Western lore, thanks mainly to the imaginative portrayals in movies, television, and even song, and perhaps due to the Western-sounding name. Some depictions are less-than-accurate versions of his life; others make only oblique references.

Ringo was played by John Ireland in the 1957 film *Gunfight at the OK Corral,* and by Myron Healy in "Johnny Ringo's Last Ride," an episode of the television series *Tombstone Territory.* Another TV series, titled *Johnny Ringo,* aired for one season in 1959–60, but cast Ringo as a lawman, which substantially stretched the truth, although he did actually serve briefly in the posse organized by Sheriff Behan to hunt down Wyatt Earp's vengeance-bent outfit.

Michael Biehn portrayed Ringo on the big screen in *Tombstone* (1993) and Norman Howell took over the role in *Wyatt Earp* (1994).

In the Geoff Aggeler novel, *Confessions of Johnny Ringo,* his name is Ringgold and he is depicted as a young man who becomes an outlaw after his betrothed was killed by Union troops in Missouri. In this version, he is killed by Wyatt Earp.

He was also the inspiration for the narrative-like recording of "Ringo," sung (or spoken) by Lorne Greene in 1964. Although historically inaccurate, the song reached the top spot on the pop charts, perhaps in part due to Greene's popularity as Ben Cartwright on television's *Bonanza*.

Two classic movies also made probable references to the real Ringo. In the original *Stagecoach* (1939), John Wayne appeared as the Ringo Kid; in the 1986 television remake, Kris Kristofferson played him. And Gregory Peck was Jimmy Ringo, a semiretired quick-draw artist, in *The Gunfighter* (1950).

And although this probably has no connection to Johnny Ringo, it is worth mentioning:

Richard Starkey, a British drummer, achieved a great deal of fame after legally changing his name to Ringo Starr and hooking up with the Beatles.

CHAPTER THREE

Curly Bill Brocius:
An Enigma of the Old West

Although history depicts him as one of the more notorious bad-men of the Old West, not much is known about either the early life or the final days of Curly Bill Brocius. That, coupled with the fact that nobody is certain if Brocius was really his family name, makes him a sort of frontier man of mystery. There is, however, complete agreement that he was not the type of person who was regularly invited over for Sunday dinner by decent folks.

He made quite a name for himself after arriving in Tombstone around 1878, and his reputation as a tough guy with few morals reached near legendary proportions before he was either killed or fled the territory in 1882. His activities during that four-year period are well documented. He killed without provocation, and legend says he would rather shoot a man for a dollar than find honest work. But where he came from and how he died remain topics for ongoing discussion and endless scrutiny.

Brocius definitely had a relationship with Wyatt Earp, and it wasn't a good one. He most certainly rode with the Clanton gang, but didn't participate in the infamous gunfight at the OK Corral. He definitely killed a lawman, but it was ruled an accident. He probably was involved in the massacre of nine Mexicans, the ambush of Virgil Earp, and the fatal shooting of Morgan Earp, but no charges were ever filed. That did not mean he was a good person.

And he may have been killed by Wyatt Earp in a shootout at Iron Springs.

Or maybe not.

There are several versions of his early days. According to one account, he was born as William Brocius in Crawfordsville, Indiana, around 1841. By the time he reached early adulthood, he was burly, dark skinned, had a head of thick, black, curly hair and was scratching out a meager existence as a farmer, barely able to support his wife and three children. When a wealthy draftee offered him a $500 bribe to join the Union Army in his place, the young man jumped at the chance and became a soldier in the Civil War. But when the conflict ended, Brocius squandered his mustering-out pay on southern belles and didn't come home as most veterans did. When he finally did show up four years later, he found his wife had married another man and had borne him a son. Brocius protested that he had been discharged far away from home and it had taken him that long to earn enough money to make it back home. Nobody believed him and he left Crawfordsville in anger, never to return.

A more interesting version is the one he told Wyatt Earp while Earp was transporting him to a Tucson jail to face a murder charge. At one point during the train ride from Tombstone, Brocius said he was a fugitive from Texas. He said he was wanted in connection with the shooting death of a government employee during an attempted holdup, but had escaped from jail on the day he was scheduled to be sentenced. And, he said, his name was really William Bresnaham, aka "Curly Bill." He had been arrested after two men attacked a military vehicle in 1878. Texas newspapers reported that one soldier was killed and another wounded. The only person identified was Robert Martin, a notorious bandit, but witnesses said the other man involved went by the name of Curly Bill. Eventually, both were arrested by Mexican authorities and returned to Texas, where they were indicted, convicted, and sentenced. But both escaped before their sentences were carried out.

After telling his story, Brocius allegedly asked Earp for the name of a lawyer who might defend him; but when Earp suggested one, Brocius said he couldn't use him because he was the attorney who had prosecuted him in El Paso.

The lawman and the outlaw were on the train together because Brocius had killed Tombstone Marshal Fred White; Earp was taking him to Tucson to stand trial. At the age of thirty-two, White had been elected the town's first marshal and took office

There are no known photographs of Curly Bill Brocius. Cave Creek artist
Bob Boze Bell painted this image based on historical descriptions.
BOB BOZE BELL, *TRUE WEST* MAGAZINE

in early 1880, just as Brocius and his gang were shooting up the town during one of their regular drunken sprees. The young lawman approached Brocius and demanded that he surrender his gun. Brocius did, but as White reached for it, the six-shooter fired, delivering a mortal wound to the marshal's abdomen.

Wyatt Earp, acting as a deputy, whacked Brocius on the head with his pistol and knocked him unconscious. White lingered for two days before succumbing to the wound. But during that time, he told authorities that the shooting was an accident, and that Brocius shouldn't be charged. Wyatt Earp testified to that effect at the trial and Brocius was acquitted.

The acquittal didn't change his lifestyle, however.

And although Earp's testimony had helped him avoid jail time, he never forgot the pistol-whipping, even though he had it coming. He and Wyatt Earp became bitter enemies, and the enmity eventually turned fatal.

Tombstone was, at that time, regarded as one of the toughest towns in the West. It got its name around 1870, when prospector Ed Schieffelin arrived from Oregon and began digging around for ore-bearing stones. The locals scoffed and told him, "The only stone you'll ever get in this country will be a tombstone." Schieffelin remembered the jibe and named his first claim "Tombstone." That one didn't reap rich rewards, but a later one in the same area did and the town grew up around it.

Typically, the lure of great wealth drew the usual assortment of miners, gamblers, outlaws, ladies wearing fancy clothing, and scam artists. Curly Bill Brocius had found a home.

Shortly after his arrival in Tombstone, Brocius hooked up with Newman "Old Man" Clanton and his "Cowboys," a band of ruthless outlaws who openly defied the law while making themselves the scourge of southeastern Arizona Territory. They wore red sashes around their necks and were held responsible for a wide variety of illegal acts. Although they were rustlers themselves, some of the Cowboys acted as tax collectors for Sheriff Johnny Behan and made other rustlers pay taxes on the cattle they stole. The elder Clanton was their supposed leader, but the gang usually operated without plan or direction; they merely used the Clanton ranch as their headquarters. Brocius drifted in and out as an unofficial member and was out of action for a while after being shot through the cheek during an argument with a companion.

Old Man Clanton was killed while trying to rustle cattle in Mexico in what became known as the Guadalupe Canyon Massacre. Brocius took over leadership of the cowboys and eventually became known as "Arizona's most famous outlaw." Under his leadership, the Cowboys grew to about four hundred members and worked both sides of the Mexican border. They stole cattle from ranches, horses from Army posts, and steers from Mexico.

They became so brazen and powerful that President James Garfield issued an order that they be stopped at all costs. It didn't produce any results. In one of their more depraved acts, the gang ambushed a Mexican mule train in Skeleton Canyon, just north of the border. The Cowboys hid in rocks above the canyon and opened fire when the muleskinners appeared below. They killed at least nine Mexicans and got away with an estimated $75,000 in loot. It didn't do them much good, however. The two Cowboys assigned to carry the stolen gold and silver had to hide it because it was too much for their horses to carry. But they were killed before they could tell the rest of the gang where it was hidden. According to the legend, the treasure is still buried somewhere in Skeleton Canyon.

Although he was directly responsible for the massacre, Brocius was never charged with any crime.

This did not mean he gave up his errant ways and became a model citizen.

His contemporaries said he was a terror with his six-gun. Some said he was able to hit running rabbits, and shoot out candle flames without damaging the candle. They also said he could shoot a quarter held between the thumb and forefinger of an unwilling volunteer, but there are no recorded instances of such an event. However, others claimed he was quick on the draw but couldn't hit anything, and was such a bad shot that some of his fellow outlaws wouldn't ride with him because they feared he might accidentally shoot them.

He was also a drunk, and a mean one.

One Sunday morning, Brocius and some companions showed up during the regular service at a church in Charleston, a mining town nine miles south of Tombstone. Still suffering the effects of a hard night's drinking the previous evening, they demanded a sermon. The parishioners fled, but the Rev. John Addison, who was conducting the ceremony, stayed and delivered an hour-long homily that warned of the awesome punishment awaiting the gunslingers. When the preacher finished with his fire-and-brimstone oration, the rowdies whipped out their guns, fired a few shots into the ceiling, and ordered him to sing a hymn. He obliged. The Cowboys then filled the collection plate and left. The clergyman also left, never to return to Charleston. Brocius was later hauled into an impromptu court and fined $50 for unlawfully interrupting church services.

In another episode, Curly Bill and some of his drinking buddies barged into a saloon frequented by Mexican laborers. They made the workmen strip to their underwear and dance while they provided the background music by firing their six-shooters at their feet.

The gang also took over an election in San Simon, a tiny railroad stop on the eastern slopes of the Chiricahua Mountains where Bob Paul and Charlie Shibell were running for sheriff of Pima County. The Cowboys supported Shibell because Paul had once ridden shotgun on Wells Fargo stagecoaches and had some run-ins with the outlaws. The town's total population was about thirty-five; only ten of them were registered voters. But when the ballot boxes were emptied, out fell 104 votes and 103 of them were for Shibell. Brocius had commandeered the voting process. He ordered every man, woman, and child to the polls and told them to cast a ballot for Shibell or else. He also gave names to all the dogs, burros, and chickens in town and, because they couldn't write, he voted for them. The election board threw the decision out and the courts eventually declared Paul the winner.

But the final chapter of the Curly Bill Brocius story was about to be written.

In March of 1882, after Virgil and Morgan Earp were shot, Wyatt decided he could not rely on local law enforcement to bring anyone to justice, so he took matters into his own hands. He intended to hunt down those he held responsible and administer his own brand of justice, which would be fatal. What followed became known as the Earp Vendetta, a shooting spree that left several suspected assassins dead.

Wyatt and Doc Holliday had taken Morgan Earp's body to Tucson, where they put it on a train headed for California. Virgil Earp, still recovering from the wounds that shattered his arm, also boarded. Wyatt had deputized both his youngest brother, Warren, and Doc Holliday, as well as hired guns John Blount (also known as "Turkey Creek Jack Johnson"), Charles "Harelip Charlie" Smith, Daniel Tipton, Texas Jack Vermillion, and Sherman McMasters to help deliver the body so it could be returned to family members in California.

As they waited at the station in Tucson, Wyatt spotted Frank Stilwell and Ike Clanton lying in ambush on a flat car. Stilwell had been named on a warrant as a suspect in the death of Morgan Earp. Wyatt moved quietly between the railroad cars and when he got close enough, he fired both barrels of his shotgun into one of the would-be assassins. Clanton escaped unharmed. When the rest of his posse arrived on the scene, they identified the dead man as Stilwell. He was the first victim of the vendetta. Wyatt and his men watched as the train carrying Morgan's corpse left, then rode out of Tucson, leaving Stilwell's body in the rail yard.

Witnesses testified that they heard several shots. One of them commented that Stilwell "was the worst shot-up man I ever saw." A coroner's inquest reported five bullet wounds in his body. The Tucson Justice of the Peace issued warrants for five of the men suspected in the shooting, but when Sheriff Johnny Behan attempted to serve them in Tombstone, they brushed him aside and rode out of town unimpeded.

The vengeance-minded group then rode into the Dragoon Mountains where they failed to find one of their suspects, but they did encounter Florentino Cruz, who allegedly had stood watch when Morgan Earp was ambushed. He also was wanted in connection with the murder of two marshals elsewhere in the territory. He died in a hail of bullets.

As the Earps continued on their deadly ride, Sheriff Behan organized a Cochise County posse to go after them. The posse consisted of about twenty ranchers and outlaws. One of his deputies was Curly Bill Brocius, who was also on the Earp hit list. Behan purposely didn't include Pima County Sheriff Bob Paul, despite the fact that the killing had taken place in his jurisdiction. Paul was a good friend of the Earps, so Behan didn't trust him.

The Behan posse got word that Wyatt and his allies had been seen in the vicinity of Iron Springs, about thirty miles northwest of Tombstone in the Whetstone Mountains. They scouted the area and discovered that the tip was correct, so they planned an ambush. As Wyatt and his crew entered a wash at Iron Springs, the posse members jumped out from behind their hiding places and began firing. Brocius was carrying a shotgun and acted as front man for the posse. He got off one shot; it tore holes into Earp's overcoat but missed him. Earp withdrew his double-barreled shotgun and let loose. Both charges hit Brocius in the chest. The blasts hurled his body against the side of the wash. Left without a leader, the other posse members hastily withdrew and there were no other human deaths.

Wyatt had several holes through his clothing but was uninjured; Vermillion's horse had been killed. The vendetta was over. The Earp posse members stayed in the area for a few more days, but with hostile posses on their trail, they crossed the border and rode into Silver City, New Mexico. They sold their horses and gear, took a stagecoach to Deming, then a train to Albuquerque. Wyatt and Holliday eventually made their way to the relative safety of Colorado.

A story in the *Albuquerque Evening Review* on May 12, 1882, reported their stay, but had a different conclusion. It noted that "... a party arrived in Albuquerque [whose] appearance in the city speedily became known among the rounders and talked about. They were men of whose deeds the whole of Arizona was ringing, the Earp boys, as they were all together spoken of. During the month before there had been hardly a day during which a cocked revolver had not been leveled at some one, seven dead cow-boys bearing witness to the accuracy of their aim . . ."

After detailing their time in town, the paper startled readers with:

Notwithstanding the fact that the newspapers did not speak of their arrival here, it became known in Arizona, and Tombstone supplied a party of man-hunters who, it appears from Arizona papers received this morning, at last found their prey. The Epitaph *gives an account of the killing of Wyatt Earp near Hooker's, Arizona, last Monday by a party which ambushed and attacked him while the Citizen indorses* [sic] *the news, adding the statement that Tipton was killed last week while with Doc Holliday. No particulars are published of the killing as both papers received their information through private sources. Wyatt met his death while returning from a visit to his wounded brother [Virgil] at Colton, California, who had but the week before assured a citizen of Tombstone that all of them would, as soon as he was well, return to Arizona and stand trial on the charges preferred against them.*

The report concluded with:

The party, while in Albuquerque, deported themselves very sensibly, performing no acts of rowdyism . . .

Later editions corrected the mistake and Wyatt Earp stayed alive until January 13, 1929, when he died of natural causes at age eighty.

Warren Earp eventually wound up in Willcox, Arizona, but did not live a long and fruitful life. In 1899, he went to work as a cowhand on a ranch near town. He didn't get along well with the ranch foreman, Johnny Boyett, and their mutual dislike came to a head on July 4, 1900, when Boyett shot and killed the youngest Earp in the Headquarter Saloon, a regular hangout for area cowboys. The shooting was reported in the next edition of *Arizona Range News*. Portions of it read:

> *Both men came into the saloon and Earp told Boyett that he [Boyett] had been offered $100 to $150 by parties in town here to kill him. Boyett denied this and told Earp he did not want any trouble, but added that if had to fight him that he was not afraid. Earp told Boyett to go get his gun, and said that he was fixed . . .*

Boyett then went next door to another saloon, took two guns from behind the bar and returned to the Headquarter. Earp saw him coming and ducked out a side door, but then came back and confronted his rival. He walked toward him, saying "you have the best of this. I have no gun." Boyett ordered him not to come any closer, but Earp continued walking toward him. The newspaper report continued:

> *Finally Boyett again repeated his warning not to advance another inch or he would shoot. Earp not heeding, Boyett fired, and Earp dropped dead.*

When deputies arrived, they found a partially opened pocket knife in Earp's hand but no gun. Boyett was arrested and had a preliminary hearing before Judge W. F. Nichols. After hearing evidence, Nichols ruled that he didn't think a grand jury would bring an indictment against Boyett, or if an indictment was brought, a jury would fail to convict him. So he dismissed the case and Boyett was freed.

A subsequent edition of the paper linked Warren Earp to the shootout at the OK Corral, noting that although he was not there when it happened, he did arrive in Tombstone shortly afterward and rode with his brother on the infamous vendetta ride.

There were rumors that Wyatt and Virgil showed up in Willcox a short time after Warren's death and Boyett mysteriously disappeared a day later. But it's only another bit of folklore. Neither of the older

Earps ever returned to Arizona, and Boyett returned to the ranch and ran it for at least another decade.

Although he never achieved the fame of his more notorious brothers, Warren Earp does have his own legacy. Every July, the city of Willcox hosts Warren Earp Days, an annual convention of Western writers. Also, a plaque commemorates his shooting on a wall in front of the former saloon (now a clothing store), and a welded steel marker stands over his grave in the city's Old Cemetery.

What happened after the death of Curly Bill was not unexpected, considering the nature of things in the Old West.

Wyatt and his companions swore that Brocius was decidedly dead, having taken two direct hits from a shotgun. However, the Cowboys claimed he was still alive, and that there had been no shootout. They claimed Curly Bill had moved to Texas, changed his name to Bill Graham and settled down. But another theory implied that the Cowboys retrieved the body and buried it in a hidden grave on a nearby ranch. Other stories circulated that he had gone to Wyoming, while some swore he had moseyed down into Mexico and married a señorita.

The numerous accounts created a kind of newspaper war. John Clum, publisher of the *Tombstone Epitaph,* accepted and printed the Earp version. But Harry Woods, publisher of the *Tombstone Nugget* and one of Sheriff Behan's deputies, openly agreed with the Cowboys' claim that Brocius was still alive and offered a $1,000 reward to anyone who brought in his dead body. Clum countered with an offer of $2,000 to anyone who produced him alive. Nobody ever stepped forward to claim either reward. Historians point out that if Brocius actually had survived, he would have leapt at the chance to ride into Tombstone and claim the $2,000 because it would have given him the last laugh in his longstanding feud with the Earps.

In the 1920s, a letter written to an unknown recipient by former Wells Fargo agent Fred Dodge appeared to shed some light on the matter. Dodge said he interviewed a Charleston saloonkeeper who told him that Johnny Barnes, a member of the team of ambushers, claimed he saw the shotgun blasts literally tear Brocius in half. According to the letter, the barkeep also said that Ike Clanton later confirmed that Brocius had been killed.

Regardless of which version was the truth, Curly Bill disappeared from the area and was never seen again.

Except in the movies, of course.

He regularly shows up on the big screen, primarily as a villain in movies about Wyatt Earp. He was portrayed by Jon Voight in *The Hour of the Gun* (1967), by Powers Boothe in *Tombstone* (1993), and by Lewis Smith in *Wyatt Earp* (1994).

CHAPTER FOUR

Ike Clanton:
Lived through OK Corral Shootout;
Died Anyway

The shooting death of Ike Clanton in 1887 was viewed by many as poetic justice. He was not a well-liked person and most who had dealings with him figured his demise was a good alternative to having him around. Besides, they said, he'd escaped with his life from the gunfight in Tombstone, so his time was up, anyway.

He might have been just another gunshot victim in the annals of the Old West had it not been for a momentary brush with infamy on October 26, 1881. On that date, Clanton achieved his spot in Western lore when he and his brother, Billy, along with brothers Tom and Frank McLaury and Billy Claiborne, squared off against the Earp brothers and John "Doc" Holliday in a confrontation on the backstreets of Tombstone.

The shootout lasted only about thirty seconds, but then took on a life of its own as the legendary "Gunfight at the OK Corral." It has since been the subject of movies, books, magazine articles, newspaper stories, and endless speculation.

Ike Clanton is a key figure in almost every account, but his role is still uncertain. Films dealing with the subject commonly take so many liberties with the truth that the truth gets lost. Ike Clanton's life is a prime example.

On the big screen, he is depicted as a bully, sniveling coward, loudmouth, drunk, cattle rustler, turncoat, informer, all around no-good, and several other characterizations, most of them less than flattering. In reality, he probably was some of those things, but not all of them. In fact, up to a point in his life, he was tolerated and even well-liked. He was a hardworking rancher who even helped lawmen make arrests a couple of times.

*Ike Clanton survived the shootout at Tombstone
but eventually became a gunshot victim.*

Regardless, Clanton is not remembered for any of his positive attributes. Rather, he is remembered solely for his participation in the infamous gunfight.

During the hail of bullets on that fateful day, the Earp brothers—Wyatt, Virgil, and Morgan—along with Doc Holliday, shot and killed the McLaury brothers and Billy Clanton. But Ike was spared after pleading with the Earps not to shoot him because he was unarmed. Wyatt allegedly told him to "go to fighting or get away." He chose the latter. Billy Claiborne, the fifth member of the Clanton group, also ran.

Although Ike later claimed that he was innocent of any wrongdoing, a story in that day's *Tombstone Epitaph* seemed to put the blame for the shootout on him. The reporter wrote:

This morning, the city marshall, V. W. Earp, arrested a cow-boy named Ike Clanton, for disorderly conduct, and he was fined twenty-five dollars and disarmed in the Justices Court. Clanton left, swearing vengeance on the sheriff and Marshall Earp and his brother Morgan, who tried to induce Clanton to leave the town. But he refused to be pacified. About three o'clock p.m., the Earp brothers and J.H. Holliday met four cow-boys, namely the two Clanton brothers and the two McLowery brothers when a lively fire commenced from the cow-boys against the three citizens. About thirty shots were fired rapidly . . .

The fight took place on a small area between a boarding house, assay office, and photography studio, not at the OK Corral, which was actually a short distance away. Due to all the conflicting reports that followed immediately—and continue to this day—there is no exact record of what actually happened during the thirty-second interval that has become legend.

According to many, Virgil Earp first ordered the Cowboys to throw up their hands and surrender their guns. But Frank McLaury and Billy Clanton drew and cocked their single-action revolvers and the shooting started. Holliday pulled the short, double-barrel shotgun from under his long coat and shoved it into Frank McLaury's midsection. But he backed off without firing. Then there were two simultaneous gun blasts. Wyatt Earp said later, "Billy Clanton leveled his pistol at me, but I did not aim at him. I knew that Frank McLaury had the reputation of being a good shot and a dangerous man, and I aimed at [him]." Once the shooting started, Holliday stepped ahead of the Earps and fired his shotgun at Tom McLaury, who reeled backward with a four-inch wound in his chest. Holliday then tossed the shotgun aside, pulled out his pistol and continued shooting at Frank McLaury and Billy Clanton. Morgan Earp fired immediately afterward, and the younger Clanton was hit in the chest and abdomen.

Although Wyatt Earp was aiming at Frank McLaury, either Morgan Earp or Holliday fired the fatal shot to Frank's head. He was hit under his right ear, and died where he fell on the street. Witnesses carried his brother, Tom, into a nearby building where he died without speaking. Billy Clanton, taken into the same building, was in considerable pain and asked for a doctor. "They have murdered me," he whispered to those standing nearby. "I have been murdered . . . Go away and let me die." He expired a short time later.

The three bodies were taken to the Ritter and Reams undertaking parlor, where they were prepared for burial, then displayed in the window over a sign that read: MURDERED IN THE STREETS OF TOMBSTONE.

The *Tombstone Nugget*'s next-day report declared:

The 26th of October, 1881, will always be marked as one of the crimson days in the annals of Tombstone, a day when blood flowed as water, and human life was held as a shuttle cock, a day to be remembered as witnessing the bloodiest and deadliest street fight that has ever occurred in this place, or probably the Territory.

An estimated three hundred people joined in the funeral procession that bore the trio to Boot Hill, and another two thousand lined the streets and watched it pass by.

All the members of the Earp faction got out of it alive, although Morgan and Virgil Earp and Doc Holliday were wounded. Initial public reaction favored them, but that changed when rumors swirled that Ike Clanton and Tom McLaury were unarmed. Then another Clanton brother, Phineas, arrived in Tombstone and claimed that the Earps and Holliday had committed murder instead of enforcing the law. A correspondent for the *San Diego Union* noted:

> *Opinion is pretty divided as to the justification of the killing. You may meet one man who will support the Earps and declare that no other course was possible to save their own lives, and the next man is just as likely to assert that there was no occasion for bloodshed, and this will be a "warm place" for the Earps hereafter . . .*

When the excitement died down, the Earps and Holliday were charged with murder but were eventually exonerated. Judge Wells Spicer, who presided over the pretrial hearings, explained:

> *In view of all the facts and circumstances of the case, considering the threats made by the character and position of the parties, and the tragical results accomplished, in manner and form as they were, with all the surrounding influences bearing upon the results of the affair, I cannot resist the conclusion that the defendants were fully justified in committing these homicides, that it was a necessary act done in the discharge of official duty.*

The coroner's jury then issued its ruling:

> *William Clanton, Frank and Thomas McLaury, came to their deaths in the town of Tombstone on October 26, 1881,*

*from the effects of pistol and gunshot wounds inflicted by
Virgil Earp, Morgan Earp, Wyatt Earp, and one—Holliday,
commonly called "Doc Holliday."*

Virgil and Morgan Earp were later shot in separate ambushes
by unknown assailants. Morgan died from his wounds; Virgil lived
but lost the use of his left arm. Many blamed the shootings on Ike
Clanton.

The suspicions were probably well-founded. Prior to the infamous shootout, the Clanton brothers, Claiborne, and the McLaurys
were all members of a gang known as "the Cowboys," an assortment of ranch hands and gunslingers who had little respect for the
law and were implicated in a wide range of criminal activity. They
were taken to task from as far away as the West Coast, where the
San Francisco Examiner editorialized that "the Cowboys [are] the
most reckless class of outlaws in that wild country . . . infinitely
worse than the ordinary robber." Although loosely organized, the
Cowboys had a strong sense of loyalty to each other because they
were either blood relatives, longtime friends, or coworkers.

The gang holed up at the Clanton ranch in Charleston, about
twelve miles west of Tombstone. It was a highly successful operation and an ideal location for their illegal activities. Because of his
drunkenness, Ike Clanton was the least popular of the four brothers who ran the ranch; brother Phineas (Fin) had been arrested
a couple of times for cattle rustling and once for robbery, but was
never convicted.

They were the sons of Newman Hayes Clanton (also known as
Old Man Clanton). Ike was born in Missouri in 1847 and named
Joseph Isaac. He was the second of seven children. The father
worked as a day laborer, gold miner, farmer, and, finally, a rancher.
The family moved into Tombstone in 1877, about a decade after
the death of Maria Sexton Clanton, the matriarch. Ike first ran a
small lunch counter, but later moved out to the ranch. It was during that time that the Cowboys organized and often were blamed
for such crimes as rustling, banditry, and murder. Despite that,

the townspeople considered most of them harmless, little more than a nuisance—all except Ike, who was widely disliked because of his big mouth.

The Clantons and the Earps were on opposite sides in almost everything. The Earps were lawmen who viewed the Clantons as habitual troublemakers at best, or outright criminals at worst. Both sides had divergent economic and political alliances and their dislikes eventually turned into hatred. Ike's bad temper and drinking problems were like gasoline on the smoldering conflict. He was loud, frequently drunk, and often boasted that in the end, he would settle matters with the Earp element to his personal satisfaction.

The longstanding rivalry came to a head in March 1881. A stagecoach robbery went wrong and two men were killed. The Earps blamed it on the Cowboys; Ike Clanton publicly declared that Doc Holliday had fired the shot that killed the driver. Holliday said he'd been playing poker in another town. Wyatt Earp then held a semisecret meeting with Ike and offered him $6,000 in reward money if he'd help capture or kill the men involved. Ike initially agreed, but then backed out of the deal.

Another situation the following June cast more splotches on Ike's reputation. According to a report in the June 9, 1881, edition of the *Epitaph:*

> *What came very near being a serious shooting affray was prevented yesterday morning by the coolness and intrepidity of Virgil Earp, acting City Marshall. Ike Clanton . . . and "Denny" McCann, a sporting man, had a difficulty in an Allen street saloon, when the latter slapped the face of the former. Clanton went out and heeled himself, and "Denny" did the same. They met in front of Wells, Fargo's office about 9 o'clock and both drew their guns about the same time, when Earp stepped between them and spoiled a good local item. They were both determined men, and but for the interference of the officer, there would doubtless have been a funeral, perhaps two.*

The situation festered and on October 25, 1881, Holliday accused Ike of lying about the stage robbery. A fistfight was averted when calmer heads intervened. But Clanton stayed in the saloon and drank all night. By noon the next day, he was seen armed with a rifle and pistol, looking for Holliday or one of the Earps.

A short time later, the historic gunfight erupted.

But the shootout didn't put an end to the animosity. Two months later, Ike and Phineas were accused of shooting Virgil Earp. Ike's hat was found at the spot where the ambushers waited on the second story of an unfinished building, but friends testified that the two were in Charleston at the time, so the case was dismissed. Morgan Earp was slain the following March. The Earps suspected Ike but no charges were ever brought. A short time later, Wyatt claimed that Ike and other Cowboys tried to ambush him and Virgil at a train depot in Tucson. The Earps were ready, however, and killed one of their assailants. Clanton and the others hustled out of town but were soon being hunted down in what became known as the Earp Vendetta Ride. Once again, Ike survived, and was now apparently safe from his hated enemies because the Earps and Holliday left Arizona Territory in 1882 and never returned.

For a while, it appeared that Ike would settle down and live out his days undisturbed, now that the Earp threat was gone. He and his brother Phineas moved up north and started ranching on land near Springerville in Apache County. But Ike couldn't leave the booze or his other bad habits behind him. He acquired a host of new enemies who considered him not only a braggart, but also a cattle thief. In an apparent effort to smooth things over with the neighbors, the Clanton brothers threw a shindig at their new ranch. Two of their guests—Lee Renfro and Isaac Ellinger—began arguing. Renfro shot Ellinger in the chest; he died four days later.

A witness said that as Ellinger lay mortally wounded, he asked the Clantons to hold Renfro and make sure he didn't get away. Ike Clanton refused, saying that Renfro was a friend. Renfro added that "these boys are friends of mine and they stand with me." The

Clantons took him along when they fled the area. That resulted in a charge of accessory to murder against Ike; the case never went to trial due to the extenuating circumstances that followed. But the dead man's father was wealthy and had powerful friends who wanted justice. They were already fed up with the Clantons' disregard for the law, particularly in the areas of cattle and horse rustling. The death of Isaac Ellinger on their ranch caused things to boil over. Now they wanted vengeance. The Apache County Growers Association, particularly angered by it all, hired Jonas V. Brighton as a private detective to bring the brothers in so they could be prosecuted.

Brighton claimed to be a Civil War veteran. He took a correspondence course to earn his private investigator license, then bought a badge and presented himself as a genuine lawman. Nobody scoffed at his lack of actual training because Brighton had the ability to work with people, to calm them down in time of crisis. This quality, the stockmen assumed, made him the ideal person to confront the Clantons.

On the night of May 31, 1887, Brighton and a special deputy sheriff were quartered in a cabin on the Jim Wilson ranch on Eagle Creek in Graham County. The next morning, as they prepared breakfast, a lone horseman approached the cabin. When the rider got within twenty yards, the lawmen realized it was Ike Clanton. According to reports filed after the incident, Clanton recognized the deputy and got a shocked look on his face, then reached down and withdrew his rifle from its scabbard. But Brighton, armed with either a large caliber pistol or shotgun, got off the first shot. Clanton reeled in his saddle; a second blast dropped him to the ground. The deadly round had slammed into his chest and probably struck his heart, lungs and major blood vessels. The other grazed his leg and would not have been fatal. There is still some dispute over which shot came first, but most agreed that Brighton had fired both. However, stories published a week later in both the *Arizona Journal Miner* and *Arizona Weekly Enterprise* said the deputy was responsible.

There was no inquest or autopsy. Clanton's reputation had turned so many people against him that his death was marked off as justifiable homicide.

The *Apache County Critic,* in its edition of June 18, 1887, made little effort to conceal where it stood in the matter when it reported:

> *It will perhaps not be uninteresting to give the readers of the* Critic *the particulars of the tragic and swift death of Ike Clanton, as related by Detective Brighton, who killed him . . . It was generally understood that the Clantons and several of their associates had drawn praises in the shape of true bills for irregularities such as horse and cattle stealing, murder, arson and most all the rest of the crimes in the long, dark catalog of felony. The finding of the indictments was brought about mainly through the clever work of Detective Brighton, and here let a note be made that to Detective Brighton, more than to any other man, is due the credit of breaking up one of the most desperate, daring and smartest gang of outlaws that ever preyed upon any community . . .*

At one point in his report, the writer referred to Ike as "poor, deluded, witty, smart and most unscrupulous," and said he was

> *a man way above mediocrity in point of native intelligence, and who, if he had an education and had chose to follow an honorable course of livelihood, would have been a leader among the honorable citizens of the territory.*
>
> *As it was, he was a leader of that class upon whose head a price is set, and who are hunted like wild animals and savages; and when you bear in mind that Ike Clanton was a leader of this sort of following, it required a bit of nerve for two men to go on the hunt of such game, in their*

wild mountain retreat, where one or two desperate and determined men would be more than a match for ten men should they be taken unaware . . .

After presenting an account of the shooting, the reporter noted that "Mr. Wilson, at whose ranch their tragedy occurred, notified the nearest neighbors and four men came over and identified the deceased and assisted in giving him as decent a burial as circumstances would admit."

He summarized Clanton's demise with this editorialized conclusion:

Thus ended the wild career of poor deluded, misguided Ike Clanton. He sowed to the wind and has harvested the whirlwind, and his harvest is gathered into a narrow house, six feet by two, and the panther, wolf and bear growl a fitting requiem over his grave. His end was typical of his life—swift, rough and the hardest that could be the fate of any mortal man. Let us hope it is for the best.

Ike Clanton was forty when he died.

Fin Clanton later surrendered and was eventually sentenced to a term in the Yuma Territorial Prison.

Ike's death meant that all five members of the so-called Clanton gang died of gunshot wounds. Tom and Frank McLaury and Billy Clanton were slain during the shootout at the OK Corral and Billy Claiborne was mortally wounded in a gunfight with Franklin Leslie in 1882.

With the exception of Morgan Earp, all members of the opposing faction died of natural causes. Doc Holliday succumbed to tuberculosis in Colorado at age thirty-six in 1887. After leaving Tombstone and escaping two attempts on his life, Virgil Earp was hired as a marshal by the Southern Pacific Railroad in California, where he died of pneumonia at age sixty-two in 1905. Wyatt Earp, the last survivor, traveled across the West for several years, accompanied by Josephine Marcus, the actress for whom he abandoned his wife. He gave lectures, became involved in real estate, did some writing and a lot of gambling. A urinary infection caused his death at the age of eighty in 1929.

But most of them live on, primarily in the movies based on the immortal shootout. Ike Clanton was portrayed by Grant Withers in *My Darling Clementine* (1946) and by Lyle Bettger in *Gunfight at the OK Corral* (1957). Robert Ryan played a sophisticated Ike in *The Hour of the Gun* (1967). Other notable depictions were by Stephen Lang in *Tombstone* (1993) and Jeff Fahey in *Wyatt Earp* (1994).

CHAPTER FIVE

Joe Boot:
The One-Hit Robber with a Female Boss

Most Western bad guys achieved their notoriety because they actually were bad men whose careers stretched over extended periods. Joe Boot was different. He had only one known criminal endeavor and it was an absolute failure. Even worse, while his accomplice went on to the big time in Western folklore, he wound up as a mere footnote in the pages of history.

Boot was involved in what was probably the last stagecoach robbery in the United States. He and his partner made off with some money but got lost during their getaway attempt and were apprehended within four days. He surrendered meekly. His partner put up a fight.

His partner was a woman.

Her name was Pearl Hart. She was the reason Joe Boot turned to a life of crime, albeit a very short one. Boot would have been better off if their paths had never crossed; Hart came out of the ill-fated episode wearing the mantle of a legend.

Their brief association began in the late 1890s, in mining camps of Arizona Territory's Pinal County. After failing as a farmer in the Midwest, Boot relocated to Arizona to try his hand at mining, a very popular trade at the time. Nobody knew much about his background. Most of his acquaintances figured Joe Boot wasn't the name his mother had given him after his birth somewhere in Ohio, sometime in the early 1870s. In fact, some historians theorize that it was an alias provided by Pearl Hart when they formed their partnership. But it didn't make much difference; a shady past was common among those who came to the West to seek their fortunes by digging up the earth.

Conversely, Pearl Hart's early days were well documented. Once she became famous as a lady bandit, both the frontier media and big-city publications launched aggressive print campaigns and scrambled all over themselves to report her story.

While digging into her past, they discovered that she had been born as Pearl Taylor in 1871, the daughter of a middle-class Canadian couple that was not wealthy, but able to afford tuition at a finishing school. She made good grades but was considered a rather wild young woman who was disrespectful of her elders. And she often made bad decisions. One of those came when she was sixteen. She eloped with Frederick Hart, a professional gambler who wasn't very good at his profession. They had a son, but Hart drank a lot and became abusive, so his teenage wife took their child and fled back to her family.

She left the son with her parents and went to Chicago where she worked in carnivals and a Wild West show. Enamored with what she thought was the romance of the Old West, she moved to Colorado, then Phoenix. There was a degree of romance, but it wasn't what she had hoped for. Instead, it usually involved clandestine meetings in seedy hotels where she exchanged her womanly charms for cash. Things got better for a short time when her husband found her in Phoenix and begged for another chance. She made another bad decision and gave him one. They had another child but, after five years of togetherness, Hart said he'd had enough with wedded life and joined the Army, leaving Pearl to again fend for herself. She went back to the meager wages she earned doing domestic chores and, probably, prostituting herself. Things went from bad to worse; she tried to kill herself on at least three occasions, but friends stopped her every time.

Miserable and distraught, she sent her daughter back to her parents and migrated to the mining camps in the Pinal Mountains east of Phoenix. Life was hard and it didn't get much easier when she received word that her mother was ill and begging her to come home. She was cooking for a mining company in Mammoth. The work was steady but the pay was minimal, so she could afford nei-

*Joe Boot was either the instigator or the accomplice
when he and Pearl Hart robbed a stagecoach.*
YUMA TERRITORIAL PRISON STATE PARK

ther to pay her way back to her mother's beside nor send money to help with medical bills.

Then she met Joe Boot.

They became friends and he convinced her that they could earn more money if they moved to Globe, a larger city and the center of mining activity. Once there, they formed a loose partnership, staked a mining claim and began digging for gold. But like most other endeavors in their relatively short lives, the venture didn't lead to either wealth or a happy ending. Their claim yielded nothing and the little money they had was rapidly vanishing. The distress was compounded when Pearl received more letters from home, each one bearing the news that her mother's health was worsening. Then a telegram arrived. It said her mother was dying; it pleaded with Pearl to come home and be at the woman's bedside in her final hours. "That drove me crazy," she said later. "I had no money. I could get no money. From what I know now, I believe I became temporarily insane."

Stranded as she was in the mountains of Arizona Territory, Pearl Hart turned to Joe Boot for help. He was as broke as she was, but said he'd think it over. A short time later, he came up with what he figured might be a possible solution: They should rob a stagecoach. She didn't think it was a very good idea. Boot was forceful. He said it would be easy; robbing stagecoaches was not considered a good source of income anymore because they no longer carried payrolls or mail. Therefore, he argued, nobody would be expecting a holdup so there wouldn't be anyone riding shotgun on the stage. The plan was foolproof, he insisted—easy and foolproof.

Pearl remained wary and uncertain. But her mother lay dying. Her mother needed her. Pearl made her decision and it was another bad one. She agreed to Boot's plan.

And so, on May 29, 1899, Pearl Hart and Joe Boot stepped outside the law.

Both fame and infamy would follow.

Pearl cut her hair short, tucked what was left under a cowboy hat, and put on some of Boot's clothing. They weren't a good fit; she stood about five-foot-two and weighed about a hundred pounds while Boot was four inches taller and weighed fifty pounds more. But she made the necessary adjustments and they rode out of Globe, heading south toward Cane Spring. Once there, they dismounted and waited. The stage departed later, carrying three passengers and Henry Bacon, the driver. When it neared Cane Spring, the coach slowed down to maneuver a sharp curve and the novice bandits pulled bandannas over their faces and struck. They drew their pistols, took aim at Bacon and yelled "Elevate!" Boot had figured it correctly. There was no shotgun-armed guard and the element of surprise was on their side.

Unaccustomed to being held up, the driver threw his hands into the air and obeyed immediately. While Boot covered him, Pearl dismounted, ordered the passengers out of the coach, and began searching them. One was chewing on what appeared to be a chaw of tobacco. When she noticed a string hanging from his jaw, Pearl ordered him to spit it out. He did. It was a tobacco sack containing $200, almost the same amount as the other two passengers were carrying. After relieving them of all their money, Pearl gave each victim a dollar so they'd have enough to buy food when they arrived in Florence.

Before mounting her horse, Pearl grabbed Bacon's six-gun. Then the robbers rode off in the proverbial cloud of dust, heading across the desert through sagebrush and creosote bush. The holdup had gone as well as could be expected, and had netted them slightly more than $400. The getaway, however, was a different story. Unskilled as they were at escaping, the two had neglected to figure out how they were going to reach Benson, where they hoped to catch a train that would take them far away from the liabilities associated with robbing a stagecoach. So they got lost and wound up riding aimlessly in circles for three days. They were nowhere near the Benson station when they sought refuge in a cave where a javelina, a type of wild peccary, had also taken up residence. Boot shot and killed the beast, and then built a fire. The novice criminals fell asleep in the hope that the next day might bring them better luck.

Pearl Hart was Joe Boot's partner in an ill-fated stagecoach holdup.
SCOTTSDALE CC SOUTHWEST STUDIES

It didn't.

Although Pearl had tried to disguise herself, Bacon recognized her and imparted that information to Pinal County Sheriff W. E. Truman when the stage arrived in Florence. The sheriff organized a posse and the chase was on. It ended on the morning of the fourth day after the robbery, when the posse found the bandits, exhausted and sound asleep. They crept into the cave without disturbing their quarry, removed their guns, and woke them up to inform them that they were under arrest. Boot gave up right away but Pearl turned on her enemies, snarling that she would have killed them if they hadn't taken her gun.

Sheriff Truman later told a reporter, "One wouldn't think that she is a very tiger for nerve and endurance. She looks feminine enough now, in the women's clothes I got for her, and one can see the touch of a tasteful woman's hand in the way she has brightened her cell. Yet, only a couple of days ago, I had a struggle with her for my life. She would have killed me in my tracks could she had got to her pistol . . ."

When news of the robbery and capture spread, Pearl Hart became an instant media celebrity, pursued by reporters from as far away as New York. This was not just any stagecoach holdup; it was the first one ever pulled off by a woman. (Although nobody realized it at the time, it would also be the last stagecoach robbery in the United States.)

But, although he had planned the robbery and was an active participant in its execution, Joe Boot received very little attention. Newspapers and the arresting officers made him the butt of frontier humor, ridiculing him as "the inept desperado with the female boss." When their cases came to a joint trial, Pearl was the focus of sensationalized newspaper stories but Boot was almost excluded in the reports. The jury found Boot guilty and sentenced him to a thirty-year term in prison. But the same jury returned a verdict of not guilty for his partner in crime. This infuriated Judge Fletcher Doan, who was presiding over the trials. He severely chastised the first panel before dismissing them, and then impaneled a new jury.

Judge Doan had Pearl rearrested and tried on a charge of theft for stealing the stage driver's six-gun during the holdup. The new panel debated for about fifteen minutes before finding her guilty. The headlines screamed the news when she received a five-year sentence; nobody said much about Boot's thirty years in confinement. Both were sent to the territorial prison at Yuma.

In those days, Yuma was not given much respect. An article in the *Arizona Sentinel*, published in the summer of 1872, declared ". . . this was the hottest place in the world; so hot that in the summertime wings melt off mosquitoes, the Indians cover in mud, the Mexicans crawl into their little huts, and the Americans stand in the river half the day and keep drunk the rest of the time to avoid death by melting."

The prison was placed in Yuma as the result of political maneuvering by Yuma County legislators who thought it would boost the city's economy. There were no architectural drawings to guide contractors in charge of building the facility because, rather than pay an architect, officials held a contest to create a design. The winner got $150. The blueprint included no ventilation and only minimal sanitary facilities. Prisoners did most of the construction work, using native stone and adobe created from Colorado River mud. The cell doors opened on July 1, 1876, when seven prisoners were incarcerated. Nobody liked it. The prisoners and reformers thought it was inhumane; the townspeople believed the prisoners had it too easy and referred to it as "the country club on the Colorado [River]."

In June 1896, the *Arizona Sentinel* lent its voice to the accusations of leniency toward the inmates by observing, "One can go any day to the prison and see convicts singing and skylarking, joking and all-in-all having a grand old time at the expense of the taxpayer. It is well known here that the prison on the hill is more a place of recreation and amusement than servitude."

There was a slim element of truth in such harsh words. Inmates could work on craft items, which they sold at bazaars held within the walls. As a result, many of them became skilled artisans, producing intricate silver jewelry, hand-carved wood inlays and delicate lace. They also had access to a library that consisted of more than

1,500 books and almost 1,400 magazines and newspapers, acquired through donations and fees collected from tours. In addition, prisoners had good drinking water while the townspeople had to deal with water polluted by poor street and garbage maintenance.

The prison also had some rather unorthodox punishments for rules infractions. For example, a convict might draw a two-day stay in solitary confinement for not bathing, three days for littering the yard, and three to ten days for gambling, but only one day for making a knife.

Although thrust into these surroundings against their will, neither Boot nor Hart seemed to suffer much during their relatively brief stays in Yuma. Hart was given such special considerations as a small yard outside her cell and unlimited visitation rights, which led to a multitude of interviews from magazines, periodicals, and newspapers all across the nation. She was hailed by some as a women's libber because, during her trial, she told a judge that she refused to obey laws that were enacted without input from her gender. She often posed for photographs, some of them showing her holding an unloaded rifle.

Hart was released after serving only three years of her five-year sentence, and under rather strange circumstances. There were rumors that she became pregnant, a situation that would have caused considerable embarrassment because if it was true, among the visitors who might have been held responsible were the warden, some guards, and Alexander Brodie, the territorial governor. There is no record that she ever had a third child; however, one of the conditions of her release was that she leave Arizona and never return.

Her departure was reported in the *Yuma Sentinel* with this account:

> *Quite a large number of people were at the depot to get a glimpse of Arizona's famous female ex-bandit and they were not disappointed for she was there, and if there is one thing more than another that Pearl is not shy on, it is a fondness for notoriety.*

She moved to Kansas City, where she shared quarters with her sister, who had written a drama about Pearl's life that would, according to the publicity, "embody Pearl's own experience as a stage robber, with all the blood and thunder accompaniments, and the famous Pearl will once again, with her trusty Winchester, hold up the driver of a Western stage, line up the passengers and relieve them of their valuables . . ."

The play, entitled *The Arizona Bandit,* actually did open in Kansas City, and then got on the Orpheum's traveling circuit. But it was not well received. One critic caustically observed that "Pearl Hart portrays herself with all the enthusiasm of a pile of rocks."

When the play closed, Pearl found work managing a cigar store in Kansas City but was arrested and charged with receiving stolen goods and running a gang of pickpockets. She was sent back to jail, but this time only briefly. Then the details of her life story get rather muddy. One version says she went to San Francisco and died there in 1925. Another account claims she moved to New York, adopted an alias and worked in Buffalo Bill's Wild West Show. When that ended, she defied the terms of her release and moved back to Arizona, where she married Calvin Bywater, a Pinal County rancher.

Clara Woody, a newspaper reporter, said she discovered Pearl on the ranch in 1940 while working as a census taker but never explained why she made the connection. Her story said the woman was "sloppily dressed" and that her house was littered with cigar butts.

Another story popular in the 1920s says Pearl returned to Florence and visited the courthouse where she had been tried and convicted. She commented, "Well, the place hasn't changed much," and when asked how she knew, she replied, "I'm Pearl Hart, the lady bandit."

Prior to all that, however, Joe Boot had settled in to prison life as inmate Number 1558. He worked his way up to the position of trusty, driving supply wagons to chain gangs laboring on projects outside the prison walls. One day he steered his wagon through the prison gate and rode off, never to be seen again. Officials believed he escaped into Mexico. He had served less than two years of his sentence.

The prison that held Joe Boot and Pearl Hart was vacated in 1909 and is now an Arizona state park. More than three thousand inmates were incarcerated behind its walls during its thirty-three years of operation. Twenty-nine of them were women. The first four female inmates were at the prison one at a time, but each was quickly pardoned because, with no one to talk to, it felt like solitary confinement.

Female prisoners created problems. The prison had been designed to hold men, so there weren't any cells for women's special needs. Therefore, other cells had to be rearranged to accommodate them. Prison officials also had to create different uniforms for the women.

Jeanie McClurry and Georgie Clifford were the first women to share a cell, and Elena Estrada and Rosie Duran were the only women to spend time in solitary after they got into a fight with each other. Although the allegations that Pearl Hart was pregnant during her time in the prison apparently were untrue, one woman prisoner did give birth there. Manuela Fimbres has that dubious distinction. She bore a son who was allowed to stay with his mother until she was released. Her pardon included the condition that she leave Arizona and never return.

And those who visit the old penitentiary today are likely to hear the rumor that there was an additional chapter to the saga of Joe Boot and Pearl Hart. According to that oft-told legend, the two were lovers in prison and, after his escape and her release, they were reunited in the mountainous regions of Pinal County and lived together until he died.

But the more common, and perhaps more factual, story is that, once parted, they never saw each other again.

Regardless of which story is true, the life of Pearl Hart ended years ago but the legend survives. She has been the subject of *The Legend of Pearl Hart,* a musical production that ran in New York in 2006. A play entitled *Lady with a Gun* was written and staged in Prescott in 2002. *Legend of Pearl Hart,* a movie, was filmed in 2007 but has not been released. She has also been the subject of countless books and historical references.

Joe Boot is rarely, if ever, mentioned in any of them.

CHAPTER SIX

The Goofy, the Bad, and the Unsuccessful:
Scammers and Bumblers Had Poor Success Rates

The pages of Arizona history are filled with outlaws, scam artists, rustlers, con men, robbers, and other persons of an unsavory nature, but not all of them are chronicled to the same extent as the more famous—or infamous, depending upon the point of view.

Many took up a life of crime only briefly, and then either rode off into the nearest prison or wound up in a boot hill before they achieved the pinnacles of their chosen profession. Others simply weren't very good at being criminals, and so they never got the notoriety of their more successful peers.

Grant Wheeler and Joe George were two classic examples of bumbling train robbers whose success rate was zero.

On January 30, 1895, the two cowpokes figured that herding cattle was no way to get rich, so they decided to hold up a Southern Pacific train, remove the contents of the safe, and live happily ever after. This being their first attempt at train robbery, they didn't have much practical experience in the art of being criminals, but they forged ahead regardless. First, they pretended to be miners and bought dynamite from a store in Willcox. Next, they stored the dynamite and hobbled their horses in some brush near a siding about seven miles out of town, then walked a couple of miles back to meet the train.

It was easy to stop the train because it had to maneuver a steep grade, which slowed it down enough so the robbers could jump aboard. Faced with a six-gun stuck in his face, the engineer willingly brought the train to a halt. The novice bandits uncoupled

Grant Wheeler tried and failed, then tried again. And failed again.
SCOTTSDALE CC SOUTHWEST STUDIES

the passenger cars, and then ordered the engineer to pull the mail and baggage car ahead to where they had stashed the explosives. Once there, they disengaged the express car and told the engineer to pull the locomotive away from the scene.

With visions of untold wealth waiting for them, the duo broke into the express car, placed the dynamite around the two safes and lit the fuses. The blast tore the door off the smaller safe but didn't harm the larger one. Assuming that the treasure was inside the big safe, they tried again, this time using more dynamite. Same result. Frustrated, the would-be robbers stuffed all their remaining explosives around the safe, and placed eight big sacks filled with coins on top to serve as ballast. They lit the fuse and hightailed it to safety. This time, it worked. The resounding blast shredded the body of the express car and blew a mixture of lumber and coins all over the countryside with such force that the coins were embedded into telephone poles and cacti.

When Wheeler and George entered the splintered car, however, they found that the safe contained only a few dollars. The real treasure was the thousands of silver Mexican pesos in the sacks they had used as ballast. They found a few before riding away in disgust. The engineer reattached what was left of the express car, drove the train back to the rest of the cars, hooked them up, and headed back to Willcox. Lawmen tried to organize a posse, but they got only a few volunteers because most of the townspeople grabbed rakes and buckets and headed for the site of the robbery.

The cowboys didn't learn their lesson, however. They tried it again less than a month later. Although their first effort had been a dismal failure, they relied on the same strategy: hold up the train, uncouple the express car, order the engineer to drive them to their dynamite cache, and blast the safe open. The attempt went as planned until they reached the rendezvous point and discovered they had unhitched the wrong car. The one carrying the money was two miles back, still coupled to the passenger cars.

Wheeler and George again rode away empty-handed. They were eventually tracked down by lawmen in Colorado. George was killed by a posse and Wheeler took his own life rather than surrender to his pursuers.

Two other robbers from that same era weren't much smarter.

During the winter of 1881, according to sketchy sheriff reports, Henry Corey and Ralph Gaines hatched a get-rich scheme that might have worked if they hadn't messed with the frigidity of Mother Nature and the determination of Arizona lawmen. The pair stole eight large gold bars from a mine near Gillette, a former camp in northeastern Arizona that is now nothing more than rubble and scant outlines of former buildings wasting away under the relentless summer sun and inhospitable winters. Each bar measured three feet long by four inches wide. Each was worth a fortune.

After pilfering the gold, the two thieves buried the bars near a cabin on Rogers Lake, then hustled back into Flagstaff where they robbed a stagecoach of an estimated $25,000 in gold and silver coins. They returned to their cabin, dug up the gold bars and placed all their loot into large wooden kegs normally used in the production of beer. Then they chopped holes into the ice covering Rogers Lake and lowered their ill-gotten wealth into the frigid waters. When the heat was off, they figured, the ice would be gone and they could easily retrieve the goods.

But Corey and Gaines hadn't counted on the determination of deputies from the Coconino County Sheriff's Office, who got word that the pair was holed up at the lake. They organized a posse and headed toward the lake. However, the robbers heard about the posse and had to leave in a hurry. Since the lake was still frozen over, they didn't have time to retrieve the loot, so they left it there. Their plan was to ditch the lawmen, hide out until spring, then return and recover the precious metals.

Their plan failed. Gaines was killed in a shootout over a card game in eastern Arizona; Corey was arrested during a botched holdup and drew a twenty-four-year prison sentence in Yuma Territorial Prison. After his release, he and an associate returned to the lake but never found the barrels. Neither has anyone else, even though the lake goes almost completely dry every summer.

Although John Heath didn't actually take part in an 1883 robbery, he nonetheless paid the full price for being involved. He helped plan the holdup of a store in Bisbee, but things didn't go as expected and three innocent citizens were gunned down by Heath's five accomplices. All five were caught and sentenced to hang, but Heath demanded a separate trial on the grounds that he had not actually participated. He got one and was sentenced to a term in the Yuma Territorial Prison.

This didn't sit well with the locals. Many felt Heath deserved the same punishment as the other five, so they organized a lynch mob, broke into the jail and strung him up on a telephone pole. The next day, Cochise County coroner Dr. George Goodfellow issued his verdict that Heath had succumbed due to "emphysema of the lungs which might have been, and probably was, caused by strangulation, self-inflicted or otherwise . . ."

Lafayette Grimes and Curtis Hawley were also victims of the lynch mob. They ambushed a pack train carrying the mail across the Pinal Mountains from Florence to Globe. Two men were killed, and an express box loaded with $5,000 in gold coins was taken. Before he died, one of the victims described the attackers to lawmen. Grimes was arrested and identified his brother, Cicero, and Hawley as coconspirators. All three were jailed in Globe.

An angry mob quickly formed. They gathered outside the jail and threatened to take the men by force if Sheriff W. W. Louther didn't surrender them. Outnumbered and outgunned, the lawman agreed, but only if the crowd would assure him that the men would get fair trials. In the hope that they might be saved from a hangman's noose, Lafayette Grimes and Hawley told the mob that they'd show them where they'd hidden the loot. Cicero Grimes was left behind and begged for mercy, telling his captors that he had only acted as a scout and was not involved in the murders. The widow of one victim also pleaded that his life be spared. When the townspeople agreed, Cicero was turned back over to the sheriff, who whisked him out of town and hid him in a cave.

The search party led by the other two suspects returned around midnight. They had found the gold divided into equal three shares, so they demanded that Cicero Grimes be turned over to them. When the sheriff refused, they turned their wrath toward the other men, who were given time to write out their wills before being marched out to an old sycamore tree. Members of the mob placed nooses around their necks but just before the ropes were tightened, Lafayette Grimes fell to his knees and removed his footwear. His last words were, "Damned if I'll die with my boots on."

Not all lynch mobs were successful. William Baldwin escaped one, thanks to the diligence and bravery of a lawman.

Baldwin was arrested near Roosevelt in 1907 and charged with murder. While Sheriff Henry Thompson was taking him back to jail, a mob formed and threatened to lynch the suspect. Thompson was able to hold them off and deposited Baldwin in the Gila County jail in Globe. Still angry, the citizens surrounded the jail and demanded that the sheriff turn the arrested man over to them so they could hang him.

Forced to act, Thompson and his deputy, Bill Voris, formulated a plan. The deputy sneaked Baldwin out a back door and the two spent the bone-chilling January night in an unheated outhouse behind a local church. Before dawn, they scurried down to Pinal Creek and hid underneath a railroad trestle. At an appointed time, Thompson and a railroad worker arrived on a two-man hand-operated railroad vehicle. They put Baldwin on board, hid him under a tarpaulin and pumped their way east. A few miles out of town, they transferred the prisoner to an eastbound passenger train and he was safely moved to the Graham County jail in Solomonville.

But the escape did Baldwin little good. A Solomonville jury found him guilty of murder and he was hanged.

Not all those who played loosely with the law came to such a harsh ending. Cleve Van Dyke was a land developer in Miami, Arizona, when the city got its first post office in 1909. When he became aware that most homeowners wanted to live near the post office, Van Dyke built a small building and called it "the Miami Post Office." It was a green structure on wheels so it could be easily moved. He would haul the mobile building to an area where he was selling lots. When the lots were all sold, he moved the Post Office to his next location.

He got away with it three times before the United States Postal Service built a permanent structure.

In 1910, Anthony Blum was on trial in a Connecticut courtroom, accused of bilking Father Arthur De Bruycker in a scheme that involved a mining operation in far-off Gleeson, Arizona Territory. The priest claimed he had given Blum $5,000 to invest in "a sure thing" out West but had received no profit from the venture because, he came to believe, there was no mine in Gleeson. His lawsuit alleged that Blum was guilty of fraud and misrepresentation.

Blum used a variety of tactics to delay the trial for more than two years. Eventually, however, he had to face the music. But while telling the court his side of the story, he suddenly pitched forward from his chair on the witness stand and collapsed. Court officials rushed him to a nearby room where his personal physician examined him and solemnly announced that there was no hope. Blum had suffered a heart attack and would be dead within minutes.

As he lay dying, Blum declared that he was a Catholic and wanted to make a final confession to a priest who could then administer the last rites. The only clergyman available on such short notice was the plaintiff, Father De Bruycker. True to his beliefs, the priest got permission from the court to enter the room, hear the man's confession, and administer the absolution. His actions, however, placed the clergyman under the seal of the confessional. He could therefore never reveal what Blum had confessed.

And suddenly, there was a miracle. Apparently, confessing his sins had given Blum the strength to recover. His doctor gave him another examination and said he was well enough to go home. The trial was put on hold for more than a year, and then the case was withdrawn because Father De Bruycker could no longer testify against Blum. The priest was also severely chastised by the higher-ups for demonstrating such poor judgment, and he never got one penny back from his $5,000 investment.

Anthony Blum faked a heart attack to avoid
prison for scamming a priest.
COURTESY OF GLENN SNOW

Blum's case wasn't the only time justice was derailed in the courtroom. A few years earlier, Rufus Nephew escaped a certain prison term when he swallowed the evidence against him.

Nephew, known as Climax Jim because of his affinity for a certain brand of chewing tobacco, was well known throughout the territory as a thief and cattle rustler. In addition, he was an expert at breaking out of jail. He often boasted that there wasn't a pokey in the Southwest that could hold him, and the *Solomonville Bulletin* described him as "the most slippery bird in the Southwest."

Despite that, he was brought to trial in Graham County on a charge of check forgery. He had allegedly sold some rustled beef to a butcher in Clifton; when the amount on the check didn't match what Nephew thought it should be, he increased the number to his satisfaction. During the trial, the prosecutor introduced the altered check as his prime piece of evidence and placed it on the table in front of Nephew and his attorney. Nephew whispered to his lawyer and told him to object. He did and a lengthy debate ensued.

When the discussion got heated, Nephew reached inside his shirt and pulled out a sack of his favorite tobacco. He set the bag down on the check, and then picked it up. Since chewing tobacco is rather moist, the check stuck to the bottom. As he was stuffing the bag back into his shirt, Nephew grabbed the check, balled it up, plopped it into his mouth and ate it. With the only evidence against him now coursing its way through his digestive system, the case against Nephew was dismissed.

Fleming Parker didn't get off that easily when he pushed a case of frontier justice beyond its limits.

Parker raised horses in the Prescott area. One day in January 1897, a train killed two of his animals and the railroad offered a settlement that he considered an insult. So he decided to take matters into his own hands by robbing a train. Days later, Parker and three friends boarded a train at Peach Springs and stole $100 in registered mail, about the amount Parker figured he had coming. One of his accomplices was shot and killed during the robbery;

Parker and the other two were captured eight days later by Yavapai County Sheriff George Ruffner.

Despite the death of one robber, public opinion was still on Parker's side because the railroad refused to settle with him. But that changed when Parker and two other inmates escaped from jail. During the break, Parker grabbed a shotgun and used it to gun down a deputy district attorney. Nobody sympathized with him anymore. Ruffner recaptured him nineteen days later and returned him to Prescott, where a jury found him guilty of murder and sentenced him to hang. Several appeals followed, but to no avail. On the morning of his execution, Parker refused a last meal. Instead, he asked for an hour with Flossie, a prostitute from the city's infamous Whiskey Row. His request was granted. An hour after that, he was dead.

Up in the White Mountains, they still talk about the way Pecos Higgins acquired his horse.

Higgins was a likable character who occasionally butchered a neighbor's beef in the still of the night, then offered the neighbor half of it the next morning. He was married five times, had a drinking problem, was arrested twice for selling liquor to Indians, and wound up in jail both times.

When asked how he got the horse he rode into Arizona, Higgins replied, "The night I left Texas, them ole boys was a-runnin' me hard and it was a stormy sonofabitch. I noticed my rope had been draggin' and when I come across the New Mexico line, I looked back and there was a fine [horse] on the end of 'er. How he got there, I don't know but I just let him stay and brought him right on through to Arizona with me."

Higgins eventually got religion and settled down before he died at age eighty.

Dick Loyd also had a drinking problem, but he didn't live long enough to overcome it.

Loyd once got drunk, stole a horse, and rode it into a Tombstone saloon where Curly Bill Brocius, Johnny Ringo, and several other nefarious characters were playing poker. Unfortunately for Loyd, the horse belonged to one of the players. Because horse theft was a serious crime, even among the bad guys, the gamblers filled Loyd with bullets. He dropped to the floor of the saloon and the killers continued playing cards, occasionally tossing some of their winnings onto the body to help defray funeral costs. Afterward, they removed the victim's shabby clothing and dressed him in a new suit, white collar and black bow tie. Brocius paid for the outfit, saying that the old clothes were good enough for riding the range, but as a corpse, he should at least be stylish and look the part.

They placed the body in a pine box and hauled it to the cemetery, where Brocius put a bottle of whiskey between Loyd's folded hands and said, "You went out like a crazy drunk but you'll have a hell of a long time to sleep it off."

The saloons in and around Yuma were once favorite hangouts for William Beck, also known as Cyclone Bill. And how he got his nickname was always a big topic for discussion.

Beck hired on with a freight company and was assigned to drive a mule team from Yuma to Tucson. His pay would be a share of the profits derived after sale of the goods. But the rig never got to Tucson, and Beck had vanished. More than a year later, he ventured into Tucson and was accosted by the owner of the freight line, who naturally demanded to know what happened.

Beck's response:

While driving through the desert about halfway between Yuma and Tucson, a cyclone descended upon the outfit and swallowed up the team, the wagon and himself and whirled them way up into the sky before plopping them back on the ground. Beck said he didn't know where he was but he followed the sun and started walking toward Tucson. It took him a year of wandering through the desert before he finally got there. Hauled into court, he told the judge that he didn't know what happened to the mules and merchandise; all he knew was that he was lucky to escape with his life. The judge didn't display any sympathy, so Beck acquired both a jail sentence and a nickname.

There weren't any libel laws in the Old West, which was fortunate for the crusading frontier newspaper publishers who pilloried and smeared their enemies with a reckless abandon similar to modern-day radio talk shows.

One of the most verbose was John Marion, editor of *The Miner* in Prescott in the mid-1860s. Marion had no equal when it came to spewing vitriolic wrath in print. A prime example was his description of Judge Sydney de Long after the two had a major falling out. Marion ran a photo of the judge and wrote underneath it:

> *his forehead is suited for flattening out tortillas; his nose projects some distance from his face and . . . his mouth appears to have been well-cut with some dull instrument, either a crevice spoon or a shovel; and the eyes—those glorious orbs—look like empty egg shells. We mean to preserve this picture by having it framed with brass and mounted on a braying ass so as to represent the pious judge in the act of blowing his trumpet . . .*

Gold and other precious metals weren't the only lures the scammers employed to separate honest folks from their money. In one con game, it was soap.

J. T. Greathouse, L. G. Greathouse, and William Duffy arrived in Thatcher in 1927, touting a grandiose undertaking that was guaranteed, in their words, to make everyone in town rich. They announced a plan to found a soap factory and soon acquired several investors. They leased space in the basement of a local building and began distributing samples of a soap they called "Silver Queen."

The samples were widely acclaimed for their quality, and soon the residents were begging for the chance to invest. The promoters said the locals would have to pay for the necessary equipment as part of their investment. Within a short time, the Gila Valley Manufacturing Company was formed. But then, the bubble burst.

In January 1928, the three men suddenly disappeared with about $54,000 of the stockholders' money, leaving behind empty promises and overpriced equipment that nobody in town knew how to operate. Warrants were issued and an investigation revealed that the soap samples were chipped from another brand—probably White King—that was already on the market. Nobody got any money back, but J. T. Greathouse was later tried and convicted in Louisiana for embezzlement. The other two thieves vanished into the pages of history.

Greed also was the undoing of Thomas F. McLean, also known as "Yuma." McLean came to Arizona Territory after being thrown out of the United States Military Academy at West Point for several violations. He bitterly renounced his white heritage and joined a band of Aravaipa Apaches, married an Apache woman, and took his new name. He also observed that tribal members paid their debts with gold nuggets and decided to use that knowledge to his advantage. He befriended a chieftain and talked him into revealing where his people got the nuggets. The chief said he'd show him the lode, but on the condition that he could make only one trip to the site and could never reveal its location. Yuma agreed, but greed overtook agreement.

Before he was killed in 1861, two years after the find, McLean allegedly returned to the mine several times, once accompanied by John D. Walker, an Indian agent. But when Yuma was killed by vengeful Apaches who clubbed McLean and his wife to death, Walker hid out and was never able to return to the site. He died in 1873, after revealing the location of the gold to John Sweeney, a blacksmith. But Sweeney died in 1876, before he was able look for the treasure. On his deathbed in Florence, he supposedly passed the secret on to Charles Brown, who wasn't very good at keeping secrets. Brown told everyone who would listen that the gold was on a large hill north of Camp Grant, and attempted to reach the gold several times, but never made it due to failing health.

As far as anyone knows, the gold (if there ever was any) is still hidden in a mountain in southeastern Arizona.

CHAPTER SEVEN

Richard C. Flower:
The Man Who Invented Spenazuma

If he had applied his talents to legitimate business operations, Richard C. Flower might have been a very wealthy man—perhaps even a multimillionaire. He was very good in whatever field he chose. He was charming, convincing, earnest, and even better, he was more than willing to share the good fortune his expertise brought him.

The problem was, whatever field he chose was illegal.

This did not bother Flower.

He was an educated man, earning a law degree from Northwestern University in 1868. But instead of practicing law, he moved to New York and became interested in getting rich in a hurry. His interests turned to medicine and that lured him into quackery. He developed and bottled "Sagwa," a concoction that he claimed would cure any ailment, from rheumatism to arthritis, from back pain to stomach ulcers, and particularly "spiritual and physical sag."

To ensure its success, he gave himself the title of Doctor Richard Flower, despite the fact that he had absolutely no medical training or experience—and despite the fact that his elixir had no medicinal value. However, it did contain substantial amounts of alcohol, so very few complained about being scammed.

But snake-oil salesmen rarely strike it rich, and Flower had ambitions to join the elite. So in 1898, he left the field of medicine and went into gold mining. But the gold wouldn't be dug from the ground. It would be lifted from the pockets of unwary investors.

While still plying his medicine scam, Flower read about gold mining opportunities in Arizona Territory. For decades, there had been rumors that huge mineral deposits lay buried under portions of the San Carlos Apache Reservation, which covered a large area that extended from the White Mountains to below the Gila River.

Dr. Richard Flower almost made millions in a phony mining scheme.
SCOTTSDALE CC SOUTHWEST STUDIES

But since the land had been deeded to the tribes by the federal government in 1871, mining operations were forbidden.

Prospectors, however, had been illegally filing claims on Apache lands and some of them produced promising ore samples. Those discoveries led to pressure on the federal government to restore at least some of the land back to the public domain. Congress buckled, and in March 1877, the southeastern tip of the reservation was restored to the public domain. It was named the Mineral Strip. Several other portions were also transferred back to the public for a variety of reasons, but most of them involved mining.

The *Graham County Guardian* heralded the congressional action, noting that a governmental inspection found that the land was "rich in gold, silver, copper and coal," and that "this is undoubtedly one of the richest pieces of mineral-bearing earth in the southwest." John J. Birdno, editor of the newspaper and a real estate speculator, would eventually become one of Flower's biggest supporters.

Flower was among those who viewed this turn of events with great interest. Although he knew nothing about mining and had never been to Arizona, he recognized an opportunity. As Graham County historian Ryder Ridgeway put it years later, "as the doctor mulled over these facts, the name Arizona suddenly spelled out in gilt-edged letters and in the fertile receptacle of his mind brewed a concoction so potent that it was to affect persons throughout the entire country."

Within days, all traces of his fake medical practice were gone, and his office door was adorned with the word "Gold." He conjured up a phony mine and called it Spenazuma, an apparent play on words because "mazuma" was a slang word for money and he wanted his investors to spend it in large amounts, investing in his nonexistent mine. He formed a corporation to sell gold mining shares in the phony enterprise and printed gold-bordered stock certificates in ten-dollar denominations, cheap enough so even the non-wealthy could share the fortune.

Flower then went to Arizona, where he bought up several mining claims in the shadow of Black Rock, a huge, isolated mass of granite rising over the landscape in Graham County. He listened enthusiastically as his guide, Bill Duncan, told him that the Apaches often referred to the huge rock as Montezuma, a god who watched over their territory. He would use that myth to his own advantage.

Next, he hired surveyors, carpenters, miners, and laborers to establish a fake mining operation and lay out a town site, which he called Spenazuma. He also hired a photographer to record work on the make-believe mines. Then he returned to New York where he produced a gold-bordered prospectus filled with photos and glorious phrasing that promised instant wealth by investing in his company, now known as the Spenazuma Gold Mining and Milling Company of New York. The prospectus, hastily distributed throughout the East and Midwest, read in part:

> *Running through the center of this property is a vein of ore one-half mile in width and two miles in length, every foot of it rich in gold, copper and silver. It is said this is the richest and largest continuous vein of ore (rich from the surface rock into the bowels of the earth) ever discovered in the world. And of this rock of which there are millions and millions of tons, yields of the precious metals $12 to the ton and upwards, and doubled in value every few feet as you tunnel into the side of the mountain on either side.*

Then he came up with another stroke of genius. He declared that Spenazuma had been an actual person, the son of legendary Aztec chieftain Montezuma. According to Flower's version of history, Spenazuma had originally found the gold but had little interest in it, so it lay hidden under the earth until Professor T. A. Halchu, a fictitious mining expert from equally fictitious Longhorn, Montana, was injected into the story. Flower claimed that Halchu had come across an old Mexican man who, on his deathbed, told him about the rich mineral deposits. The dying man said they lay beneath a rock formation that resembled Spenazuma's profile. He called it Black Rock.

Flower used the story when he bought full-page newspaper ads and hired pitchmen to promote the wonders of the phony mine. They concentrated on small towns, using lantern slides to illustrate their spiels. The pictures, however, didn't depict Flower's mines; they were photos taken at legitimate operations. The unscrupulous salesmen were very successful. In less than a year, unwitting buyers invested more than three million dollars in worthless stock. Flower manipulated them even more by declaring an early dividend, claiming that the stock had risen from $12 to $15 per share.

And the *Graham County Guardian* was completely taken in. On July 22, 1898, the paper reported that thirty-five men were working day and night to dig out the gold-bearing ore, and added that equipment and building materials were arriving at the mine site daily. By September, the paper was publishing reports that a dry good store, two saloons, a meat market, a boarding house, and a Chinese restaurant were already under construction. Even better, the story claimed, "A grand ball was given at this place last Thursday evening in the new mill house. About 150 people participated and enjoyed themselves immensely. It was the grandest social event in the history of the camp and will long be remembered . . ."

Not surprisingly, the stories were not firsthand accounts. They were based on claims being made by mine officials employed by Flower.

Back in New York, Flower implemented another phase of his plan. He established a board of directors, composed of cronies and men who didn't exist. The board, according to Flower, went on a personal mission to inspect the mining operation and came back with a glowing report that boasted, in part:

a few months ago, this camp was the center of the vastness of the wild uninhabited country; today it is a city of white tents. If there was ever a spot on earth especially for a great mining camp, it is this Spenazuma Valley . . . We found this great mining property richer, greater and more valuable than ever claimed by the [company] in their prospectus.

Camp Spenazuma

Dr. Richard Flower's fake Spenazuma Mine was located near Black Rock in southeastern Arizona.

The fake assessment proclaimed that the easily mined ore-bearing dirt was worth as much as $24 per ton and would soon rise to $150 per ton, then concluded with:

[You can] dig anywhere for two or three feet and expose a rich body of ore.

Still not content, Flower next selected a group of rich Easterners to accompany him to Spenazuma, hoping that they'd buy stock and, because of their prominence, would unknowingly influence others to invest. The potential suckers rode the train and carriages from New York to Geronimo, a small territorial community a few miles west of the fake mine, where they were greeted by Apaches, teamsters, and local prospectors. The group boarded two fully furnished coaches then headed for the potential bonanza. About halfway there, Flower yelled, "Holdup!" and fired his pistol in the direction of a rock pile alongside the road. Naturally, this alarmed his guests. But it alarmed Flower even more because there were no bandits. As part of his plan, the ex-doctor had ordered two of his henchmen to stage a bogus holdup to give the Easterners a little taste of the West. When they didn't show up at the appointed time and place, Flower had to tell a fib and say he had shot at a coyote.

When the coaches arrived at the site, they were greeted by mining sights and sounds: blasting noises echoing through the canyons, sweaty miners cursing as they hauled the mineral deposits from below, and loads of supposedly rich ore being hauled away. Flower treated his guests to a sumptuous lunch, and then showed them around, pointing out the new machinery ready to be installed, the newly laid building foundations, and the partially dug tunnels. Then he invited each member of the group to grab a handful of ore samples. They eagerly complied, unaware that the ore had been purchased from other mines, then spiced with liberal amounts of gold dust as another part of the ruse.

Planting gold in ore samples was a common practice at the time. Known as "salting," it was an inexpensive hoax because a few ounces of gold, if used properly, could indicate an astonishingly rich deposit of the precious metal. So Flower knew that when the samples were assayed, the gullible investors would be completely duped into believing they were on the verge of becoming extremely wealthy.

When the caravan returned to Geronimo, Flower sent a multitude of telegrams back to his Eastern contacts, informing them that they'd have no trouble disposing of the rest of the phony stock now that the fat cats were on board. And Flower was so confident that his dreams of living the good life were about to come true that he planned to issue an additional ten million dollars' worth of stock.

But his well-laid plan was about to unravel.

He hadn't counted on George H. Smalley.

In 1897, two years before Flower arrived with his grandiose scheme, officials were becoming increasingly concerned about the number of fraudulent mining operations springing up across the territory. Buckey O'Neill, a prominent Prescott resident, suggested that because the frauds were destroying confidence in legitimate mining, an agency should be established to monitor the industry. He proposed a mining department to the *Arizona Republican*, which was then a small daily newspaper published in Phoenix. The paper brought pressure on legislators to approve the plan; it was implemented and the *Republican* established a mining beat. Reporter George Smalley was assigned to cover it, and his duties included riding over miles of sparsely populated acreage to write about the practice of digging up the earth in search of precious metals.

In the spring of 1899, while en route to a mine site near San Carlos, Smalley met Duncan, now a disgruntled former Spenazuma employee. Duncan readily told him about Flower's sham operation and volunteered to lead him to the mine. It was only about a week after Flower had hosted the Eastern investors, but when the reporter and his informant arrived, they found that all the activity had mysteriously stopped.

"There were a few men at work, but the superintendent was lounging in a hammock beneath a sycamore tree," Smalley would later write. "We were informed that the property was not open to the inspection of strangers . . ."

Determined to get the full story, Smalley and Duncan found a way onto the property and explored several of the mine shafts. He instantly discovered Spenazuma was not anywhere near the image Flower had been portraying as a place where riches lay upon on the ground, just waiting to be exploited. They examined four tunnels and three shafts and found none of them extended beyond a few hundred feet. The building frameworks that were supposed to hold the machinery were built of two-by-fours and "presented a ridiculous contrast to the massive structures legitimate companies use for housing ore crushers and concentrators," Smalley said in his report. "Work had been abandoned . . . for it had served its purpose during the easterners' visit."

Smalley spent several days interviewing local mine superintendents until he peeled back the layers of deception and uncovered the truth. He learned not only that the Spenazuma ore had been salted, but also that it wasn't even from the Spenazuma. His research revealed that claim owners from several area digs had sold ore to Flower, who packed it onto his own site. One owner told the reporter that Flower bought ore from him, then had it shipped directly back to New York and put on display in his office so potential investors could see what they were buying, even though none of them knew anything about mining.

Further, his report stated, the only commercial ore found in the entire complex was a two-foot vein of sulfide. "No copper, no gold, or silver—just lead," he wrote.

While Smalley was gathering information and writing preliminary reports, Flower continued his scam back on the East Coast. He issued more bogus assay reports that further exaggerated Spenazuma's wealth potential, and the investors who had visited the site continued their high praise by issuing an affidavit that said, in part:

most of us considered the prospectus a fairy tale [but] candidly confess that is not only true, but our own eyes have seen much

more than has been claimed, and we sincerely believe the prop-
erty to be the most valuable of its kind in the country [and] we
shall cheerfully recommend this enterprise to our friends as a
safe investment, and a rare chance for making money.

Flower used the affidavit as promotional material, accompanied by phony certificates from the phony Spenazuma Mining and Milling Co., Assay and Chemical Laboratories. The assay report confirmed the fabulous riches waiting to be taken from below ground. The report estimated the ore production profits at between $2,500 and $10,000 per day.

But it all came crashing down on May 17, 1899, the day the *Arizona Republican* published Smalley's expose under the headline: "A Tenderfoot Trap."

In the story, Smalley revealed the fake mine's location and how Flower had employed legitimate miners to pack ore to his site so investors would be fooled. He reported that Flower had erected several tents and bunkhouses to further the image of a bustling camp, and that he paid the fake miners three dollars a day, even if they never saw mineral-bearing ore.

His story quoted one miner extensively. "This is the laziest camp I ever struck," the man told the reporter. "We have a good time during our shift and very little work is done. The boss don't seem to care as long as we are in the workings, and that we not fail to work hard when anyone shows up at the shaft or tunnel where work is being done."

When the Eastern investors arrived, the man said, they were ordered to act excited and show great interest as they examined the ore samples as they were hauled out. He said the men pointed to a vein of mica at the bottom of one shaft and told the potential investors that it was gold ore.

Smalley wrote that Flower and his company were "committing a crime against Arizona which its people should punish. They are obtaining money under false pretenses, and at the same time, injuring the mining interests of the entire territory." He concluded his story with:

It is such schemes as this which hold Arizona back and place her resources before the world in a wrong light. The company will no doubt fail and hundreds of investors will hold Arizona responsible for their own folly.

Once Smalley's report was published, it was all over for Flower and the Spenazuma. Stock in his company fell to zero value and those who tried to recoup their losses were left holding worthless sheets of paper. In a desperate effort to save his outlandish scheme, Flower contacted an Arizona attorney and ordered him to offer Smalley a $5,000 bribe if he would retract his findings and publish stories declaring that he had been wrong, and that the Spenazuma was as rich as represented. Smalley refused.

Aware that bribery wasn't going to work, the attorney threatened the newspaper with a $100,000 libel suit, declaring that "unsubstantiated reporting caused his clients unbearable stress and considerable loss of income." The paper's managers defied the threat and the lawyer backed down. Territorial governor N. O. Murphy then pounded the proverbial last nail into Flower's coffin when he issued an official proclamation warning Easterners against investing in the Spenazuma Mining Company.

Even Birdno, who had staunchly defended Flower in his *Guardian* editorials, had to admit to gullibility. He was forced to admit that the mining camp was deserted and the stocks offered through advertising in his own newspaper weren't worth anything.

The scandal also had a negative effect on the local economy. Relying on the fraudulent claims, businesses had sprung up, merchandise orders flourished, and bank deposits rose drastically. Once Flower's scheme was exposed, many of those elements vanished.

But Flower wouldn't go down for the count. Less than a month later, he organized another sham mining operation on the west slope of the Pinaleno Mountains, and called it the Lone Pine Mining Company. But once again, he was exposed by Smalley's reports and left Arizona for good.

The experience in the Old West didn't bring about any drastic changes in Flower's behavior, however. Using a variety of aliases and scams, he became one of the foremost swindlers in American history. He was indicted in New York in March 1903 on charges of defrauding a woman of $50,000 in another mining scam. He jumped bail and went to Philadelphia, where he developed a scheme to manufacture telephone poles from clay. He did serve two years in prison after convincing a wealthy New York widow to invest one million dollars in one of his phony enterprises, but that still didn't stop him. He was arrested twice more, but jumped bail bonds of $25,000 both times.

The end came in 1916, after he was arrested in Toronto following a search that covered much of North America and parts of South America. While out on bail, he died of heart failure in New Jersey.

As an ironic footnote, one of Flower's original associates also tried his hand at fleecing the unwary.

As the Spenazuma scam was being formulated, Thomas McInery was listed as one of the directors, then later as the mine superintendent. When that bubble burst, McInery stayed in Graham County and, in 1900, began buying up a large number of mining claims. Once he had acquired as many as he needed, McInery began calling himself Captain Tom McInery and began publicizing his plan to drill a tunnel into the bowels of the Graham Mountains. This would, he claimed, expose the rich mineral deposits hidden in the mountains, and also create a series of reservoirs that would impound enough mountain water to irrigate the entire Gila Valley.

He named the project the Mammoth Tunnel and began drilling in 1902. He told prospective investors that he had already secured fifty million dollars in capitalization and mineral rights to 4,800 acres, but never got a chance to sell any stock. In 1908, a series of newly enacted mining laws exposed his tunnel as an enormous hoax. McInerny fled the area and was never heard from again.

Smalley left the Phoenix newspaper shortly afterward and started his own weekly publication in Tucson. When that folded, he left Arizona and briefly worked for newspapers in Los Angeles and

San Francisco. He returned to Arizona and worked as a political appointee in a variety of offices, including a position with the Federal Food Administration during World War I, then as the state's Fair Price commissioner. Later in life, he sold life insurance. He died in Tucson in 1956, and was elected posthumously to the Arizona Newspaper Hall of Fame in 1966.

CHAPTER EIGHT

Charles P. Stanton:
A Murderer but Never Convicted

During its better days, Stanton was home to about two thousand rugged individuals who operated stage stations, gold mines, saloons, and supply stores. It had a post office, justice of the peace, deputy sheriff, and restaurants. But that was before the turn of the twentieth century, back in the 1870s. Nobody lives there any more. These days, only amateur gold miners and curious folks who like to poke around in ghost towns and abandoned mines go near Stanton.

Most of them are familiar with the town's bloody history; few realize that the bones of Charles P. Stanton, the man responsible for much of it, lie in an unmarked grave hidden in a desolate canyon. Stanton was not liked during his lifetime and was not mourned after his death.

The citizenry considered him responsible for murder, theft, fraud, and a variety of other crimes. But Stanton was arrested only twice and was never convicted of anything, basically because he hired someone else to carry out his vile deeds and heinous activities.

Like most of his contemporaries, Stanton came to town (it was called Antelope Springs at the time) with a strong desire to get rich. He had migrated to America from his native Ireland sometime around 1864 and was granted citizenship in 1872. In the interim, he headed west and wound up in Wickenburg, Arizona Territory, where he found work as an assayer and gemologist for the fabled Vulture Mine. Rumors about his shady dealings were already commonplace. Allegations circulated that he had been involved in a fake diamond scheme in Wyoming, and that he was stealing from the miners while assaying their gold dust. Going back even further, there were indications that he had been expelled from an English college for theft and actions of an immoral nature.

Antelope Station was a small boom town on a slow downhill slide when Stanton got there around 1870. It had sprung up near Antelope Creek at the base of Rich Hill, so called because in 1863, a miner came across a field of gold nuggets lying on the ground. Eventually, he and his partners hauled about $100,000 worth of gold from the claim. Stanton wanted in on such easy money.

But the gold strike had petered out before his arrival. The town still had a stamp mill, boarding house, and a few hastily built structures that served as residences. Those who had toughed it out clung to the hope of finding more of the gold that supposedly lay hidden in the surrounding hills. In 1875, they petitioned for a post office and when it was granted, Stanton was elected postmaster. Within months, he also became a deputy sheriff and justice of the peace. Once he assumed all those positions, and because the US Postal Service didn't like long names like Antelope Station, Stanton had enough authority to rename the town after himself.

Although he was now in a position of power, none of his three positions paid much, and Stanton was greedy. He wanted to go into business. But there was a problem: All the good business opportunities had already been secured by others. Stanton didn't let that stop him.

He opened a general store and lunch stop, but didn't do well. Potential customers rarely came back after discovering that he was crude, rude, and in general not very likable. They preferred the merchandise offered by his two chief rivals, G. H. "Yaqui" Wilson, who ran another general store, and William Partridge, owner of the stage station. They competed against Stanton and themselves for the dollars left by travelers from Prescott, Phoenix, and several smaller communities. Wilson raised his own hogs so he always had fresh meat to offer the hungry passengers. He was also a master distiller and his home brew slaked the thirst of the dust-covered stagecoach riders.

But when the stage lines added some improvements to Partridge's stop, many of Wilson's customers deserted him. This heightened an already intense competition between the two. Stan-

Charles Stanton (center) took time out from his nefarious activities to pose with fellow citizens.

COURTESY OF LOST DUTCH MINING ASSOCIATION

ton watched and made plans to use the rivalry to his own benefit. He became friendly with both men, and then devised a plot to get rid of them.

Wilson's pigs were a major bone of contention between him and Partridge because they not only provided Wilson with fresh meat for his customers, but also created an odious atmosphere that permeated the entire community. The stench was awful but Wilson claimed it was a legitimate side effect of his business. The situation worsened and finally boiled over one night when the hogs either escaped from their pens or were let loose, more than likely by Stanton. They ran rampant through the town and finally snorted their way into Partridge's house. Naturally, this angered Partridge.

Stanton saw his chance and went to work. He approached Wilson and told him he'd better apologize and pay for the damages his livestock had incurred at Partridge's home or there'd be trouble. A short time later, he went to Partridge and warned him that Wilson was gunning for him. But Wilson had no intention of shooting his rival. Instead, he walked to Partridge's home bent upon apologizing and paying up. He never got the chance. Partridge had armed himself with a rifle and, as Wilson came toward him, he fired a single shot that killed his competition. Instantly aware that his longtime enemy wasn't armed, Partridge fled into the desert. Stanton followed and convinced the fugitive that his only chance was to surrender because the desert was a harsh place and he'd most certainly die out there.

Partridge listened to his supposed friend. But once he was arrested and charged, Stanton willingly appeared as a prosecution witness at the trial, and his testimony helped get a conviction for second-degree murder. Partridge claimed that Wilson had clubbed him with a sledgehammer so he shot him in self-defense. But the presiding judge ruled that nobody could testify about the deadly relationship between the two; Partridge's entire defense was prohibited and he never had a chance for acquittal.

Partridge was handed a life sentence in the infamous Yuma Territorial Prison. Fortunately for him, public opinion was on his

Charles Stanton's former store now serves as the office for the Lost Dutchman Mining Association.
SAM LOWE PHOTO

side and friends began lobbying state officials for a pardon. They were successful and Governor John Fremont issued the pardon on January 19, 1880, three years after the trial. Partridge then moved to Prescott where he lived quietly until his death in 1899. In his later years, Partridge claimed that he was frequently haunted by Wilson's ghost. He was buried in a Prescott cemetery under a tombstone that incorrectly spelled his name as "Patridge."

With Wilson dead and Partridge in prison, Stanton figured his plan had worked perfectly. He could take over both their operations. But he hadn't counted on John Timmerman and Barney Martin.

After the trial, an investigation revealed that Timmerman was Wilson's silent partner, so he assumed full ownership of the store. And Partridge had creditors who sold the station to Martin. Stanton's well-laid plan had failed, at least for the time being. His thought process remained the same, however, and his determination never wavered because he still wasn't as rich as he had hoped. But now he realized he would need some help to achieve his goals.

By this time, neither Stanton nor the town named after him had very good reputations. A newspaper story said the residents "liked to drink blood, eat fried rattlesnakes and fight mountain lions." And Stanton was being accused of everything from murder to child molestation.

But a few miles away, another mining camp named Weaver was populated by people with even fewer morals than Stanton's. It was a cesspool of humanity, a place so bad that, by comparison, it made Stanton look like a Sunday school. Its first inhabitants were miners working placer claims on Rich Hill. They left when the claims played out, and were soon replaced by thugs and cutthroats with few or no redeeming qualities. Aware of that, Stanton rode to Weaver in search of qualified assistants to help him continue his unholy scheme, which now meant getting rid of Timmerman and Martin. He found some excellent candidates. One of them was Francisco Vega.

Next, Stanton lied his way into another false friendship, this time with Timmerman. He offered to help with the bookkeeping and Timmerman, a newcomer to both the area and the business world, readily accepted. His trust was a fatal mistake. Stanton didn't want friends; he wanted money and power. So when Timmerman revealed that he had to make a trip to Wickenburg, and that he was carrying a substantial amount of gold dust with him, Stanton put the next step of his plan into action. Timmerman never got to Wickenburg. Juan Ruibal, one of Vega's henchmen, met him along the road and put a bullet through his heart, then stole his gold and tried to burn the body. Later, he split the loot with Stanton, who not only had ordered the murder but also had watched it from a nearby vantage point.

A short time after that murder, Stanton was arrested and charged with theft of a gold specimen. He called it a conspiracy against him, and wrote a long rambling letter to the *Arizona Miner,* alleging that top Yavapai County officials were trying to either frame him for murder or have him killed.

His letter began:

I beg that you will be pleased to give me space in your columns to expose a black and most infamous conspiracy concocted, plotted, and carried out with the most consummate skill and precision, by a powerful combination of unscrupulous parties, who hesitate not at all the perpetration of every enormity to fully accomplish their diabolical purpose, and to more effectually and completely circumvent the public, made the authorities and Territory of Arizona an unconscious participator in the plot.

He added that the sheriff himself said the accusation was trumped up in an effort to hold him while authorities hunted up enough evidence to charge him with the murder of Timmerman. He wrote that Nicanora Rodrigues, another prisoner, had been offered a deal: If he would testify that Stanton killed Timmerman, Rodrigues would be set free. Stanton said that when Rodrigues was returned to his cell, he revealed what the lawmen had offered and even recounted it "in his [Rodrigues's] own words." Stanton's version:

They [the lawmen] said to me, that man Stanton is a bad man, he is an educated scoundrel, he knows everything, he has a nerve as cool as iron, he is a dead shot, and an escaped convict. He could put on his moccasins and travel over that country faster than a deer, he knows every inch of the country, could have gone down there [ten miles to the spot where Timmerman was killed] and been back home in less than no time; he is the man that killed Timmerman and you know it, you know the bullet came out of his gun, and if you will swear to it, you will at once get out of jail and be well paid for your trouble. Will you do it?

According to Stanton's letter, Rodrigues refused the generous offer, saying, "No, I cannot do that. That man is innocent, I know he is. I am bad enough, but I cannot swear against an innocent man . . ."

The rambling letter continued that after Rodrigues was mysteriously freed on bail, Juan Ruibal told Stanton that he (Ruibal) and Rodrigues had murdered Timmerman. But Stanton, quite naturally, made no reference to the fact that he had hired Ruibal to kill the victim. However, Stanton wrote, because Ruibal turned state's evidence against Rodrigues, he was spared the death penalty and sentenced to life in prison. Of course, Rodrigues had already fled the area and was never caught.

As to the matter of the stolen gold, Stanton claimed that it had actually been stolen from his mine, and produced written statements supporting his contention. After a preliminary hearing, he was set free. He concluded his letter with a parting shot:

> *It is to be regretted that Prescott, the Capitol of the Territory, should be refuge of every precarious vagabond who can with impunity, raid therefrom, on any part of the country, and pound with the average ferocity of the hyena, upon any selected victim who invariably is a respected citizen, who finds himself in the short space of 24 hours, emblazoned by those rapacious vampires as a notorious bad man. In Justice to myself, I could not keep this from the public longer.*

Free to go back to his scheming ways, Stanton targeted Barney Martin, the only man left in his way as he tried to gain control of the entire community. He waited for the right moment, then struck.

In August of 1886, Martin and his wife and their two sons were reported missing after leaving Weaver in a wagon and heading for Phoenix. Martin was carrying $4,000 in gold from the sale of his ranch. He sold out in disgust after his barn and his house were burned down, allegedly by Stanton or his gang. So the Martins were leaving for a new beginning in Phoenix. Three weeks later, the bad news came. The entire family had been massacred. Their bodies were found near an area known as Black Tanks along the Agua Fria River. The murderers had set their bodies on fire and cut the throat of one of their horses. They had been dead for almost three weeks. Lawmen from both Yavapai and Maricopa counties formed posses and officials offered rewards of more than $2,200 for the capture of the killers.

Eventually, an unidentified man was arrested and charged with the murders, but the big news came a short time later when Maricopa County authorities arrested Stanton for complicity in the massacre. As soon as his arrest became public knowledge, the residents of Stanton began relating their suspicions that their town boss had arranged several other unsolved deaths and disappearances.

Many believed he was behind the fire that destroyed a rancher's property after the rancher refused to buy supplies from his store. They suggested that Stanton watched as a huge grass fire snuffed out the rancher's entire herd of cattle, and that he was also behind another intentionally set blaze that forced two other cattlemen to relocate their herds. When a storekeeper lost all his merchandise to yet another fire, Stanton was the first one on the scene. And they noted that he and the vicious Francisco Vega had formed a suspicious alliance.

Once again, Stanton denied all the accusations, and his lawyer said Stanton was cooperating with authorities as proof of his innocence. The area newspapers had a field day. The *Prescott Courier,* which leaned toward the Democratic Party, editorialized that because Stanton was a Republican, the case demonstrated that Republicans in general were lacking in character. Republican papers like the *Phoenix Herald* responded by pointing out that D. W. Dilda, who had been convicted of murder and hanged earlier that year, was a Democrat. More stories about Stanton's involvement began making the rounds. One of Vega's men confessed that Stanton had hired him and other members of the Vega gang to murder the family. Then a woman who often cooked for the outlaws claimed that during a drunken spree, Vega himself not only boasted about killing the Martins, but went into gruesome details about how they did it. But none of the allegations were strong enough to tie Stanton to the murders. He made an initial court appearance and was freed because, the judge said, there was no concrete evidence connecting him to the Martin slayings. The *Phoenix Herald* theorized that he had probably been framed by the New York Stock and Water Company, an Eastern conglomerate that was upset because Stanton had refused to sell them the rights to a spring he owned.

But Stanton had other troubles, caused by his affinity for young girls. He had been chased from one home by a shotgun-toting mother for allegedly molesting her daughter. Girls said to have been victims of his debauchery disappeared; other refused to talk about the incidents because they feared for their lives. Pedro Lucero's sister, a fourteen-year-old, was among those who had survived an attack by Stanton. Her brothers wanted vengeance, and they almost got it when Pedro took a shot at Stanton, but the bullet only grazed his ear. Stanton offered a $5,000 reward for his assailant, dead or alive. Also, as justice of the peace, he issued a warrant for the entire town of Weaver, assuming the tactic would nab the Lucero brothers. When that failed, he had their sixty-year-old father arrested, jailed, and beaten.

But the Lucero brothers would have the final word.

Justice was unofficially served on the night of November 13, 1886. Stanton and a friend were drinking in his establishment when three men entered. Stanton didn't recognize them as the Luceros. It was the last mistake he'd ever make. One of them pulled his gun and fired. Stanton was dead before his body hit the floor. His companion returned fire and killed one of the brothers; the other two fled on horseback. As they rode out of town, they encountered Tom Pierson, one of Stanton's enemies, and told him what had just happened. Pierson summed up the unspoken feelings of the townspeople when he responded, "You don't need to pull out. If you stick around, they'll give you a reward."

There was no search party or posse, and local authorities didn't even bother with an inquest. Stanton's body was unceremoniously hauled out of town and buried in a nearby canyon because the residents didn't want anything to do with him ever again. In his book *Lonesome Walls,* author Tom Barkdull gives a vivid account of the burial:

> *On a scorching, gluey day in the early fall of 1886, seven men labored silently up Antelope Wash, pausing frequently to mop their brows and gaze back at the village below. Six of these were clad in the rough attire of miners. Their burden was in a rough pine box nailed securely around the remains of a tyrant. The seventh man, dressed in black, walked at the rear and carried only a Bible. Thus the bullet riddled body of Chuck Stanton was transported as far as practicable from the town he had terrorized, buried deep in the ground he had drenched with blood . . .*

At about the same time, reports circulated that Vega had been shot and killed while attempting to hold up a stage.

And the crime rate in Stanton took an immediate drop.

Within four years, however, the town was on its last legs. It was renamed Antelope Springs, but the population dwindled to around two hundred. The post office closed in 1890 when the mines finally shut down, then reopened for a while in 1894 but was shuttered for good in 1905.

The boom town became a ghost town. Part of it was sold to the *Saturday Evening Post* by a descendant of one of the original inhabitants. The magazine used it as a contest prize. The winner's name is lost in the pages of history. The rest of the town site and a few aged and decrepit buildings were purchased by the Lost Dutchman Mining Association in 1978.

Only three of the original buildings are standing. One is Charles P. Stanton's old store, the site of his demise. It now serves as a recreation hall and those who enter will notice the spot where a shelf once hung. Despite what Western movies depict, saloons didn't usually have tables and chairs situated around the room. Instead, the customers stood around the periphery, facing the center, with their drinks behind them on a shelf. That way, they could watch each other as well as anyone who came through the doors.

The association has made some improvements and opened what's left of the town to gold panners, inquisitive tourists, and motor home drivers.

CHAPTER NINE

Sofia Treadway Reavis:
The Baroness of Arizona

The life story of Sofia Treadway resembles a fairy tale that doesn't have a fairy tale ending. She did meet the handsome prince who rescued her from poverty. She did get carried away into a royal lifestyle. She did wine and dine in the finest restaurants. She did consort with dignitaries, reside in a castle, and travel to far and distant lands.

But, unlike Cinderella, she didn't live happily ever after.

In the end, much of her life was all a lie. Actually, it was more than one lie. It was an extended series of lies, well conceived and brilliantly executed. She was caught up in them, swept away by them, and accepted them, primarily because her prince was a persuasive con man of the highest caliber.

Her early life remains a mystery. She probably led a relatively normal life in California as either the daughter or the ward of a rancher and his Native American wife. Or she may have been an orphan, working for the rancher as a domestic servant. Either way, her life changed drastically in 1887 when, as a young woman, she met her Prince Charming.

His name was James Addison Reavis.

He was not a nice man.

If ever the time arrives when con men and scam artists are glorified with their own Hall of Fame, James Addison Reavis will be among the first inductees. He was a man of many talents, but most of them were beneficial only to him but extremely harmful to others. He was a liar, thief, cheat, manipulator, forger, swindler, Army deserter, counterfeiter, and extortionist. He was also clever, brazen, ambitious, and silver-tongued. Eventually, he would combine all these skills to become, for a short time, one of the richest men in America.

Sofia Treadway Reavis lived the life of a noblewoman—for a while.
SCOTTSDALE CC SOUTHWEST STUDIES

And Sofia Treadway would go along for the ride to the top, as well as the plunge to the bottom.

Reavis had already established himself as an unprincipled self-promoter by the time he and Sofia met. Beginning in 1871, he embarked on a scheme that gradually gave him control over an area in Arizona and New Mexico that was larger than New Jersey and Delaware combined. During that time, he rubbed elbows with royalty, counseled politicians, blackmailed the rich, robbed the poor, and became a world-renowned financial genius.

As with most fairy tales, both the real and the fictional, this one had humble beginnings. Some researchers say Sofia was born in 1872, others say it was 1864. And there is little concrete information about her early life except that she was poor.

The story of James Addison Reavis, on the other hand, is well documented. He was born in Missouri on May 10, 1843. Fenton Reavis, his father, was an itinerant laborer. Maria, his mother, was a daydreaming woman of Spanish descent. She told her son fanciful stories in which she claimed to be the daughter of Spanish royalty and, she said, that same royal blood now flowed through his veins. It was, she told him repeatedly, his right to reclaim that heritage. Maria Reavis was also a strong supporter of the Confederacy, and when the Civil War broke out, she insisted that young James join the ranks of the Gray because she viewed the Yankees as crude and vulgar cretins whose sole purpose in fighting the war was to steal her family property. She envisioned a victory for the South, at which time she assumed the family would be elevated into the lifestyle she had imagined for so many years.

Although he did join the Confederate Army, young James didn't share his mother's enthusiasm for the anticipated triumph by the South. He got bored easily, and soon discovered he had other talents beyond soldiering. One was forgery. He started by forging overnight passes for himself and his buddies, then moved on to extended furlough passes and later to requisition papers for military equipment and supplies that he sold to local merchants so he could afford the furloughs.

When he became aware that the South wasn't going to win, Reavis deserted and joined the Union forces. Changing the color of his uniform didn't slow him down, but his sloppiness did. He got caught forging northern commanders' signatures, so he left the Blue the same way he'd departed from the Gray: in the still of the night and without mentioning it to any of his superiors.

He went to Brazil for a while, and then returned to Missouri where he worked as a streetcar conductor in St. Louis, then as a real estate agent. During that period, he found a new use for one of his primary skills when he forged an old deed on faded paper, then used the fake document to sell off some land he didn't own. When nobody complained, Reavis set out on the path that would lead to monetary and momentary riches.

His mission got a major boost in 1871, when he met Dr. George Willing, a snake-oil salesman who also peddled rotgut whiskey to thirsty, and gullible, citizens. Willing claimed he had in his possession a land grant worth millions out in the Arizona Territory. The phony doctor said he'd acquired the grant from a desperately poor old Mexican man named Miguel Peralta, in exchange for a few supplies. Although he didn't believe Willing, Reavis was intrigued. Such grants, if they were real, were still being honored by the United States government under the 1848 Treaty of Guadalupe Hidalgo, as long as they were issued before the federal government took control over much of the Southwest under the terms of the treaty and the Gadsden Purchase. Willing needed a partner and insisted that if the aged deeds could be validated, they would own more than two thousand square miles of prime real estate.

Reavis listened. He could easily apply his forging skills to such a project. He and his new partner worked on the scam for more than two years before a financial disaster in 1873 ended his career in real estate. He closed his office, left St. Louis, and decided to concentrate on the Peralta deeds. This kept him very busy for the next fifteen years. During that time, Willing died and Reavis coerced his family into giving him the old papers. He moved to San Francisco, got a job with a newspaper, and wound up scamming

*James Reavis married Sofia and turned her
into a phony heiress and noblewoman.*
SCOTTSDALE CC SOUTHWEST STUDIES

some railroad tycoons by convincing them that if his phony deeds were approved, he could help the railroads gain right-of-way privileges across what would become his property. The railroaders were skeptical, but gave him $2,000 to begin the necessary legwork and paperwork.

Next, he went to the Arizona Territory and began researching land grants, particularly how to get them approved under suspicious circumstances. Then he went to Prescott and conned Willing's family out of the deeds that had been left untouched since the phony doctor's demise. The writing on the documents was faded and barely legible, the witnesses to the alleged exchange were two itinerants, and the agreement was signed three years before Willing arrived in the territory. None of that bothered Reavis. He viewed them as a gold mine, and set his grandiose plan in motion.

Reavis was patient and thorough. Working steadily and stealthily, he created a fictionalized scenario that went back to the early 1700s. He started by making frequent trips to Mexico to study old documents. He removed some of them and forged copies, then returned the originals to avoid suspicion. He experimented with various types of paper, ink, wax seals, language, titles, and other items vital to his scheme. When he finished, he had created the Peralta family, high-born Spaniards who had accumulated substantial wealth in the 1600s under the leadership of Don Miguel Peralta. He gave them titles and moved some of them to Mexico where they were to oversee some of Spain's conquered lands. He forged birth certificates and land grants, promoted nonexistent soldiers, and drew up phony wills to make sure that all the family's riches were passed down to "the heirs of the Barony of Arizonac."

In his fake history, he claimed that when the elder Don Miguel died at age 116, his estate and wealth was passed on to a son who married a Mexican noblewoman. They had a daughter and named her Sofia, but never moved to the alleged family holdings in Arizona due to Indian uprisings and the Civil War. Then, according to Reavis, the family fortunes collapsed and the younger Don Miguel lost everything, leaving him an impoverished old man, the same poor old man who allegedly traded his deeds to Dr. Willing. And one of those deeds was the Peralta grant that Reavis would use to launch himself into infamy.

Loaded down with forgeries and fakes, Reavis filed his claim in Tucson in 1882. It had grown from the original two thousand square miles that he and Dr. Willing had settled upon to a piece of land that measured 75 miles by 250 miles, a total of 18,750 square miles that stretched from Phoenix to Silver City in New Mexico Territory. Reavis therefore claimed that he owned mountains, deserts, forests, mines, farms, ranches, Phoenix, railroads, and several small towns. The Surveyor General was skeptical, but due to an overflow of legitimate claims, the office didn't have time to thoroughly examine the Reavis documents. The con man wasn't worried. He left his phony papers at the office and moved to San Francisco to implement another step in his scheme. There, he got a job with the *San Francisco Examiner* and the owner, George Hearst, let him write and published anonymous stories that promoted the Peralta grant. Although there was hardly any truth in the articles, they helped Reavis acquire investors for his land grab.

Reavis returned to Tucson a few months later, accompanied by two henchmen. They hauled several more fake documents into the surveyor general's office and demanded that Joseph Robbins, the man in charge, examine them immediately. As he studied the phony papers, Robbins grew concerned. It appeared that the claims might be legitimate.

The plan was working. Reavis began extracting payments and rental monies from mine owners and farmers, ranchers and railroads. He hired gunmen to threaten his "tenants" to either pay rent or move out. He began shaking down large companies who had set up business on lands he claimed to own. The Silver King Mining Company, which was producing more than six million dollars a year, readily surrendered $25,000 in blackmail money.

Reavis became rich, and with wealth came bravado. Those who resisted his claims were threatened with brute force, intimidation and, if that didn't work, violence. They were beaten, had their livestock stolen and their homes destroyed.

Eventually, however, his victims rose up against him. Territorial newspapers made Reavis a prime target and local governments started looking closely at his land grant papers. Tom Weedin, publisher of the *Florence Enterprise*, climbed aboard the anti-Reavis bandwagon with unlimited enthusiasm. He accused Reavis of extortion, bribery, and other crimes, and his editorials became so relentless that Reavis went to his office and offered him a bribe to lay off. When Weedin refused, his office was vandalized. Reavis claimed he was not involved, but the attack resulted in even more vigorous accusations by other frontier newspapers.

Then in 1884, Territorial Attorney General Clark Churchill filed suit to further explore the land grant claim. When the hearings began, Reavis launched a counterattack. He produced legitimate letters and documents signed by railroad and mine owners that said they had willingly complied with his requests. Some of the letters even declared that the writers had invested their own money in his get-rich schemes. The case dragged on for a year before Churchill gave up. Reavis was free to continue.

And he got even bolder.

He contacted Sen. Roscoe Conkling of New York and convinced the lawmaker that the federal government should keep its nose out of his business. Conkling agreed and became a Reavis ally. Back in Arizona, Reavis and his hired guns were going about their illegal enterprises with no interference from any governmental agency. He used some of his investors' money to build a huge ranch spread near Casa Grande and named it Arizola.

But then things started going sour. The Democrats won the 1884 election and President Grover Cleveland appointed a new surveyor general for Arizona Territory. His name was Royal Johnson and he was determined to bring Reavis down. He started by releasing a lengthy study that branded the Peralta land grant a fake. His report carried substantial weight. The word spread, all across Arizona and back to Washington, D.C. Reavis was finished. His scheme collapsed and he fled to California.

Under ordinary circumstances, that would have been the end of the Reavis story. But James Reavis wasn't an ordinary man. He wasn't done. He'd be back, this time with the one person who could prove his claim.

Her name was Sofia Treadway.

During his hiatus in California, Reavis went back to work. He figured the best way to regain control of his ill-gotten land was to become legally tied to it, so he invented more Peralta family members. In this new version, twins were born to a Peralta heiress and her shiftless husband, who were living in California at the time. He deserted the family. One twin and the mother died shortly after childbirth; the other twin was placed in the care of John Treadway, the California rancher. In this rendition, Reavis and the girl met on a train and he remarked that she looked a lot like Dona Sofia, the imaginary last known Peralta heir. They formed a friendship and, according to Reavis, he was astounded when he realized that she actually *was* Dona Sofia's very own daughter, which made her heir to the family fortune that Reavis had just manufactured out of thin air. According to this fictionalized account, the two fell in love and were married.

At this point, there was one thread of truth woven into the tightly-knit pattern of deception. In reality, Reavis actually did meet Sofia on a train and did comment on her resemblance to the fictional Dona Sofia. He claimed he had met the mother in California several years before, another fabrication because he was in the Confederate Army at the time. Before long, he was telling young Sofia that the resemblance was too strong to be ignored, and that she more than likely was the daughter of a wealthy Spanish heiress. Eventually, he convinced her that she was also an heiress, and that he could help her claim her fortunes. Either too young or too naive to realize that she was being duped, or too enamored with the prospect of becoming rich, Sofia Treadway agreed to become a part of his duplicity.

Reavis was clever and patient. He sent his new partner to a convent in San Luis Rey where the nuns instructed her in the basic skills of a high-born woman and, equally important, provided her with social graces so she could acquire the culture and poise they'd need to associate with the politicians and royalty he planned to meet as part of his manipulations.

He also changed her name from Sofia Treadway to Dona Carmelita Sofia Micaela de Peralta, the Baroness of Arizona.

While she was at school, Reavis went to a church in San Bernardino and tricked a priest into giving him access to parish birth records. Then he erased two entries and replaced them with the names of his fake Peralta twins. Fortunately for Arizona, but unfortunately for Reavis, the church kept a second set of birth records that he didn't know about. It was a rare mistake that would cost him later.

When the nuns deemed his protégée ready for high society, Reavis married her. And since his wife was a baroness, Reavis automatically became a baron. He began calling himself the Baron de Peralta, also known as the Baron of Arizona.

Now outfitted with a phony "legitimate" Peralta descendant and hundreds of phony documents to prove that she was what he said she was, Reavis filed new claims in Tucson, then took his new bride to San Francisco where he told a newspaper reporter that he was doing it for all for his wife. He said he had no interest in her claims, but that it was his duty "to see that her rights are given her." Next they went to Spain where they were treated like royalty. They used Sofia's well-crafted fake nobility to gain audiences with the courts as well as the national archives, where Reavis once more put his talents to use by forging more documents to bolster his ambitions. He also scoured the streets for flea markets, where he bought old pictures of unknown persons that he could pass off as his wife's distant relatives. The former Sofia Treadway was living like a princess. She and her husband went to England and hobnobbed with Queen Victoria, even representing the phony Barony of Arizonac at her Golden Jubilee celebration.

But then came trouble. When they returned to Arizona, the couple was made fully aware that nobody liked them. They were rich, but they were despised. An editorial in the *Tucson Citizen* suggested that the solution to the Reavis situation was "a tall tree and a long rope." More political changes brought Reavis back under federal scrutiny. Royal Johnson, who had labeled the claims fraudulent years earlier, was back on the job as surveyor general. He called the grant "fraudulent," absolutely worthless," and "utter fiction." There were flaws in many of his documents. He had used the wrong wording in some cases, the wrong writing instruments in others. Johnson cited misspellings, signs of erasures, write-overs, paste-ups, and other alterations.

Faced with evidence that no jury could deny, Reavis reacted in typical fashion—he sued the federal government for eleven million dollars, claiming that the accusations had ruined his livelihood. But it was all in vain. The feds had too much evidence against him. Sofia could only stand by and watch as prosecutors developed their strong case against her husband.

The tide had turned. Reavis was losing both in and out of court. His business associates stopped bankrolling him and his friends deserted him. When his case came to court, the onetime millionaire couldn't afford an attorney and had to defend himself. He was a better con man than a lawyer. He was found guilty. His sentence included two years in prison and a $5,000 fine, which he couldn't pay.

Despite being down and out, Reavis still wasn't finished. After his release from prison in 1898, he again sought investors for new land development schemes. But this time, nobody listened. As he grew older, he wandered the streets of Phoenix or spent hours in the public library, reading newspaper accounts of his days as a rich man. He spent his last years on a poor farm in Downey, California, where he had once taught school.

And Sofia, no longer a baroness but now a destitute single mother raising the twins she bore Reavis and the son they adopted, sued for divorce on the grounds of desertion and nonsupport. She moved to

Denver where her sons grew up without ever knowing their father. The twins served in the armed forces during World War I. In her final days, she earned some income by selling her story to newspapers and magazines. She died in 1934, about twenty years after the death of her former husband, the onetime Baron of Arizona.

Sofia Treadway was portrayed on both the big and little screens, by Ida Lupino in the movie *The Baron of Arizona,* and by Anna Navarro twice on the television series *Death Valley Days*.

Today, only a concrete marker sitting on a roadside south of Casa Grande shows where Reavis built Arizola, a spread that was once larger than the current city.

CHAPTER TEN

Ernesto Miranda:
Those Seven Famous Words Didn't Save Him

On the night of January 31, 1976, a young Hispanic man was fatally stabbed during a fight in a Phoenix bar. He had been playing cards and drinking with two other men when the altercation started, allegedly over some coins lying on the table. The police were called in. Considering the location, it was a relatively routine call. They placed the wounded man in an ambulance but he was dead before the emergency vehicle reached the hospital.

The incident didn't get much attention, even when the victim's identity was released. It was Ernesto Miranda. He was a convicted felon who had been in and out of prison for twenty years. In view of the circumstances, there was nothing very noteworthy about that. But it became a front-page story when someone pointed out that the dead man was the same Ernesto Miranda who unintentionally became the reason behind those seven words made famous by televised crime dramas:

"You have the right to remain silent."

His confession under police interrogation was the basis for *Miranda v. Arizona,* a landmark United States Supreme Court case. In 1966, the nation's highest judicial body ruled that anyone suspected of criminal activity must be informed of their right to consult with an attorney before they are questioned by police, and of their right to remain silent to avoid self-incrimination. The decision became known as the Miranda Warning. It is still in force.

Ernesto Miranda was an unlikely candidate for such a high-profile legal decision. He had a troubled childhood, frequent brushes with the law as a young adult, then convictions as a rapist, kidnapper, and armed robber. When apprehended and

Ernesto Miranda's trouble with the law resulted in the Miranda Warning.
SCOTTSDALE CC SOUTHWEST STUDIES

questioned about one of the most serious charges, he made a written confession that was the key piece of evidence introduced by the prosecution during his trial.

It would also turn out to be the major factor in the Supreme Court decision.

The journey leading up to that point began in the mid-1950s. Miranda's early years gave every indication that he was destined for a life of crime. He was born on March 9, 1941, and got into trouble for petty crimes while still in grade school. His first criminal conviction occurred when, as an eighth grader, he was charged with felony burglary then released on probation. The next year, when he should have been a freshman in high school, he was convicted of burglary and sentenced to a one-year term in the Arizona State Industrial School for Boys.

He served his time and went free, but not for long. A month later, he was back in the reform school, this time charged with attempted rape and assault. After his second release two years later, he moved to Los Angeles. The change in scenery didn't alter his lifestyle. Within months, Miranda and the Los Angeles Police Department became well acquainted, but it wasn't a warm and friendly relationship. He was arrested on suspicion of armed robbery and several minor sex offenses. The armed robbery charge didn't stick but the sex accusations did; he was convicted and served thirty months in jail. No longer willing to deal with the troublesome teen, the state of California ordered him out of its boundaries and shipped him back to Arizona.

Now eighteen years old, with an unsavory history and not much hope for a better future, Miranda decided to join the US Army. That didn't work out well, either. He was in uniform for only fifteen months. During that time, he went absent without leave several times, and was charged with voyeurism for spying on the sexual activities of others. The AWOL and peeping tom accusations led to more time behind bars: six months at hard labor in the stockade at Fort Campbell, Kentucky. He was also ordered to see a psychiatrist, but attended only one session. The army grew tired of his repeated offenses and got rid of him via a dishonorable discharge.

His mother had died when Miranda was young and his father remarried. That arrangement didn't sit well with the teenager and the relationship became strained to the point where Miranda had little to do with his father, stepmother, or brothers. So when the army busted him out of the service, he had no place to go, no place he could call home and feel accepted. As a result, he became a drifter. He wandered through the South on a path that eventually led him back to the familiar surroundings of the jail cell. Authorities in Texas gave him time in the slammer for living on the street with no permanent address. Police in Tennessee arrested him for driving a stolen car, which resulted in a federal prison term because he had driven the stolen car across state lines. He served 366 days in penitentiaries at Chillicothe, Ohio, and Lompoc, California.

Now barely twenty-one and the owner of a lengthy criminal record, Miranda apparently tried settling down for a while. Following his release from Lompoc, he met Twila Hoffman, a twenty-nine-year-old mother of two who was separated from her husband but trying to scrape together enough money to divorce him. They moved in together and after the birth of their daughter a year later, Miranda moved the family back to his hometown of Mesa, where they both found employment. She worked at a preschool nursery; he was hired by a Phoenix produce company to work nights on a loading dock.

And Miranda's name stayed off police blotters for a while.

But it was a brief sojourn.

In March 1963, he was arrested on suspicion of kidnapping and raping a young Phoenix woman, and during the ensuing investigation, police discovered that he most definitely had not turned away from his life of crime and become a model citizen. In fact, their findings revealed that he had been involved in at least two similar incidents before being caught. On November 29, 1962, he allegedly abducted a young bank teller in downtown Phoenix, forcing her into his car while holding a knife to her throat. While

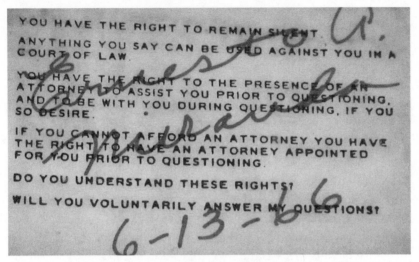

*After his various convictions, Ernesto Miranda sold
autographed copies of the law bearing his name.*
SCOTTSDALE CC SOUTHWEST STUDIES

he fumbled around trying to remove her blouse, she begged him
not to hurt her and offered him the money in her purse. He ran
his hand inside her thigh, then took the money and released the
victim. Less than three months later, on February 22, 1963, an
eighteen-year-old woman was grabbed by a person she described
as "a young, slightly built Hispanic man." He forced her into his
car and tried to rip her clothing off but fled when she screamed.
Eight days after that, the investigators claimed, he did commit an
actual rape. The victim, another eighteen-year-old, was walking
home from a bus stop in north Phoenix when he forced her into his
car and sexually assaulted her.

But this time, he wouldn't get away with it.

The police were particularly intent on solving the case because
rape was becoming a major problem for Phoenix. There were 152
sexual assaults in the city in the year prior to this attack, up 20
percent from the previous year and up 33 percent from 1961.

A short time after starting their investigation, the police got
a major break. The victim and her brother-in-law were waiting

at the same bus stop when they spotted a car similar to the one driven by the rapist. It slowed down, long enough for the pair to get a license plate number. But they read the number wrong; the number belonged to a car that could not possibly be involved. However, police shuffled the numbers and traced them to a 1953 Packard that belonged to a Mesa woman. Her name was Twila Hoffman. When Phoenix police officers Carroll Cooley and Wilfred Young contacted her, she said the car was hers, and that she often lent it to Ernesto Miranda, her live-in boyfriend and the father of her third child. She said Miranda was home, but asleep. She woke him and he agreed to accompany the officers downtown. Because he fit the description provided by the last victim, and because of his lengthy record, he became their prime suspect.

Once downtown, Miranda was placed in a lineup and two of his alleged victims identified him as their attacker. Still unaware that he had been fingered, he asked what the charges against him were. The arresting officers implied that he had positively been identified but didn't tell him what the crime was. He was then escorted into an interrogation room where detectives questioned him for more than two hours without informing him of his rights. The cops told him that two victims had identified him; Miranda shrugged and said he might as well confess. When they came out of the room, the lawmen were holding the handwritten, signed statement and added that the suspect had also admitted the two earlier attempts but hadn't written them into his confession. Next, they brought his last victim to the station and arranged a meeting with Miranda for positive identification. She said his voice matched her attacker's; he admitted that she was the woman he had assaulted. The police had no doubt that they had the right man and he was formally charged.

Miranda had written his confession on a legal pad. It had certifications typed across the top of each page that said "this statement has been made voluntarily and of my own free will, with no threats, coercion or promises of immunity and with full knowledge of my legal rights, understanding any statement I make can and will be used against me."

But nobody informed him of his right to have an attorney present while he was being questioned. Or that he could choose to remain silent.

The trial took place in mid-June of 1963 and went smoothly for the prosecution, primarily due to the signed confession. Gary K. Nelson, Arizona assistant attorney general, headed the prosecution team. Alvin Moore was appointed as Miranda's defense attorney and objected strenuously to the introduction of the confession as evidence, but was overruled by Maricopa County Superior Court Judge Yale McFate, who was hearing the case. He also allowed the jury to consider the officers' testimony about the oral confession.

The prosecution presented only four witnesses: the victim, her sister, and the two police officers. The defense called no witnesses, instead concentrating on cross-examination. Moore contended that the victim showed no bruises or cuts to indicate that she had fought off her attacker. Then he prodded the detectives into admitting that Miranda was never told he could seek advice from an attorney before entering the interrogation room.

None of it made any difference. Miranda was convicted of rape and kidnapping and the sentence was twenty to thirty years on both counts, to be served concurrently. Moore appealed to the Arizona Supreme Court; the verdict was upheld.

Two years after being imprisoned, Miranda filed a request asking the US Supreme Court to review his case. Moore, his court-appointed attorney, was now seventy-five years old and not in good health so he was unable to represent his former client. This prompted the Arizona branch of the American Civil Liberties Union, through ACLU attorney Robert J. Corcoran, to involve itself in the case. Corcoran asked Phoenix attorneys John J. Flynn, John P. Frank, and Peter D. Baird to represent Miranda. The methods of police interrogation were about to be altered.

The lawyers wrote a 2,500-word petition claiming that Miranda's Fifth Amendment rights had been violated during the interrogation, then sent the petition to the US Supreme Court in January

1966. The highest court in the land agreed to hear the case, along with two others of a similar nature, to clear up a variety of misunderstandings created by an earlier ruling titled *Escobedo v. Illinois*. After confessing to a murder during questioning, Danny Escobedo changed his mind and said he wanted a lawyer. When the court uncovered evidence that showed officers had been trained to ignore the rights of suspects during questioning, it ruled that his confession could not be used against him. The ruling in that case declared, in part:

> *Under the circumstances of this case, where a police investigation is no longer a general inquiry into an unsolved crime but has begun to focus on a particular suspect in police custody who has been refused an opportunity to consult with his counsel and who has not been warned of his constitutional right to keep silent, the accused has been denied the assistance of counsel in violation of the Sixth and Fourteenth Amendments, and no statement extracted by the police during the interrogation may be used against him at a trial . . .*

Also considered at the same time was *Mapp v. Ohio,* a case in which police entered Dollree Mapp's home in Cleveland, looking for someone else. They didn't find the suspect but they did find obscene materials so they arrested Ms. Mapp. The case was thrown out because they didn't have a warrant to search for the smutty literature.

Both those cases were heard first. When their turn came, Flynn and Frank stated that Miranda had not been advised of his right to remain silent when he had been arrested and questioned, and that because Miranda was emotionally disturbed and had a limited education, he could not be expected to understand his Fifth Amendment right not to incriminate himself.

Nelson, speaking for the state of Arizona, told the court that forcing police to advise suspects of their rights would seriously obstruct public safety and jeopardize future police investigations.

The high court reviewed the petition and, by a five-to-four vote, ruled in Miranda's favor. Voting for the majority were Chief Justice Earl Warren, Hugo Black, William Brennan, William Douglas, and Abe Fortas. Dissenting were Tom Clark, John Marshall Harlan, Potter Stewart, and Byron White. Warren wrote the majority opinion, which was released on June 13, 1966. It read, in part, that because the accused "has been refused an opportunity to consult with his counsel and who has not been warned of his constitutional right to keep silent, the accused has been denied the assistance of counsel in violation of the Sixth and Fourteenth Amendments, and no statement extracted by the police during the interrogation may be used against him at a trial . . ."

The opinion also noted that it was rendered in order to combat the "inherently compelling pressures which work to undermine the individual's will to resist [during an in-custody interrogation] . . . [and] to permit a full opportunity to exercise the privilege against self-incrimination, the accused must be adequately and effectively apprised of his rights and the exercise of those rights must be fully honored."

The court also maintained that a defendant's right against self-incrimination has always been a part of the country's justice system, and said that if it was not implemented, the result could lead to government abuse. The court supported that opinion by citing the high evidence of police violence designed to coerce, or force, confessions.

"The defendant's right to an attorney is an equally fundamental right, because the presence of an attorney in interrogation enables [him] under otherwise compelling circumstances to tell his story without fear, effectively, and in a way that eliminates the evils in the interrogations process," Warren wrote. Without the fundamental rights, he added, no statement obtained from the defendant can truly be the product of his free choice.

Warren concluded with the now-famous phrase, "You have the right to remain silent."

But if Miranda thought the ruling meant he was going to be free to resume his criminal lifestyle, he had it figured all wrong.

Although the high court had ruled that his rights had definitely been violated, the decision didn't automatically result in a ticket out of prison because the result of the failure to inform him of his rights did not automatically result in a "get out of jail free" card. Instead, it meant he'd get a new trial during which his confession could not be used against him. But, while laboring under the assumption that he would be set free, Miranda got into a dispute with Hoffman over custody of their daughter. She became angry, then fearful, and contacted police. She told them that Miranda had confessed his crimes to her and that she would be willing to testify against him.

So when Miranda got the new trial, it didn't make any difference.

Even without his written statement as evidence, nothing changed. The second trial began on February 15, 1967, after a lengthy hearing in chambers. At issue was whether Hoffman, as a common-law wife, could testify against Miranda. Maricopa County Attorney Robert Corbin said she could. Flynn, now representing Miranda, bitterly disagreed. After hearing both sides, Judge Lawrence Wren ruled the testimony was admissible. Hoffman was allowed to take the stand and her words were devastating. Miranda was again found guilty and given the same sentence.

While Miranda was back in prison, police departments around the country began issuing Miranda Warning cards to their officers and informing them that they must recite the card's text to any and all suspects while making an arrest. With a few minor alterations, the cards typically read:

You have the right to remain silent. If you give up that right, anything you say can and will be used against you in a court of law. You have the right to an attorney and to have an attorney present during questioning. If you cannot afford an attorney, one will be provided to you at no cost. During any questioning, you may decide at any time to exercise these rights, not answer any questions or make any statements. Do you understand these rights as I have read them to you?

Miranda served only a portion of his sentence and was released on parole in 1972. Hoffman and their daughter were no longer a part of his life. He supported himself by selling autographed Miranda Warning cards for $1.50. He was also able to use his namesake ruling to defend himself several times over the next four years when he was arrested for illegal possession of a gun and numerous minor driving offenses. The gun charge was dropped, but because carrying a firearm was a violation of his parole, he was sent back to prison for another year.

Not much changed after his next release, either. He was working as a delivery truck driver and was never arrested again, but he spent most of his off hours in seedy bars and inexpensive hotels in the rougher sections of Phoenix. He was playing cards in one of them, La Amapola Bar, on January 31, 1976. His playing partners were two illegal immigrants from Mexico. One was Fernando Rodriguez; the other was identified in police reports only as Moreno. The fight broke out; Miranda received the lethal stab wound. According to police reports, Rodriguez had given Moreno a six-inch knife and told him to "finish it with this."

After the stabbing, Moreno, the alleged killer, raced from the scene and ran down an alley. Rodriguez was arrested and read his rights. He elected to remain silent and was released because authorities didn't have enough evidence to hold him. Neither man was ever seen again, and police assumed they had fled to Mexico. The case was closed without anyone ever being charged.

Miranda had been stabbed twice, once in the chest and once in the abdomen. He died in the ambulance. He was thirty-four years old.

Among the items police found on his body were several Miranda Warning cards, each autographed by Ernesto Miranda.

The La Amapola Bar was torn down in the 1970s, the victim of a downtown Phoenix urban renewal project. So were most of the other buildings that once constituted "the Deuce," an assortment of flophouses, porno theaters, and bars where the economically challenged could buy liquid sustenance for fifty cents.

The Miranda Decision was seriously challenged almost a quarter of a century later when Congress enacted a statute that allowed a voluntary confession to be admitted as evidence. The Supreme Court reviewed the statute and declared that it was an "invalid attempt to change the result of the Miranda case." By a seven-to-two vote, the high court held that the Miranda warning requirement was based on the US Constitution and that Congress had no business trying to alter it through legislation. As a result, the Miranda warnings still must be given beforehand in order for a statement of a defendant to be admitted during a trial.

CHAPTER ELEVEN
Randy Greenawalt:
A Killer without Remorse

The small crowd gathered outside the walls of the Arizona State Prison in Florence knew there was no hope for a stay of execution. But they came anyway, some to protest capital punishment, and some to make sure Randy Greenawalt got what he deserved. He had avoided this moment for almost twenty years. Now, on January 23, 1997, the final chapter in his life was about to be written.

Greenawalt was going to be the seventh man executed in Arizona since reinstatement of the death penalty in 1976. He was charged with several crimes, including murder and aiding and abetting a prison escape. He was involved in at least five killings.

Nobody was going to feel bad when the prison guards strapped him to a gurney and doctors administered the lethal injection. The murderer of Theresa Tyson was finally going to pay. It would be short and swift, not like the horror he inflicted upon some of his victims.

Of course, he had maintained, it wasn't entirely his fault. The truck driver, for instance. He died because another trucker had offended Greenawalt many years before. And the families he killed later had to be taken care of because they were threats to his freedom. But none of that mattered anymore. All the customary appeals had been filed. Some were upheld, but in the end, it didn't make any difference. It was January 23, 1997, and a particular form of justice was about to be carried out.

Prison officials made the announcement. Randy Greenawalt was dead. The crowd dispersed. Many of them would return to Florence and protest the twenty-one executions that would follow. Their presence saved no one.

Greenawalt's body was placed in a plain casket furnished by the prison. After a brief ceremony, he was buried in the prison cemetery. He was about two months shy of his forty-eighth birthday.

*Randy Greenawalt was executed for his part in
a murderous prison escape.*
ARIZONA DEPARTMENT OF CORRECTIONS

Ironically, Greenawalt might still be in prison serving a life sentence if he hadn't met Gary Tison. In 1974, he was convicted of killing a trucker who was sleeping in the cab of his rig at a rest stop along Interstate 40 near Winslow. He drew an "X" on the door of the cab near the victim's head, then stepped back and fired a round through it. He later confessed to killing another trucker in Arkansas, and a man in Colorado. He shot the truckers, he said, because one of them had "roughed him up" several years before.

Gary Tison was also a lifer. The Casa Grande native, married and the father of three sons, was no stranger to life behind bars. His father had been a convicted felon, and Gary was imprisoned at age twenty-five for robbery, but escaped from the Pinal County jail during a meeting with his wife, Dorothy. He was recaptured, then paroled, but arrested again for parole violation in 1967 when he tried to pass a bad check. In April of that year, while being led to a court hearing, Tison overpowered a prison guard, handcuffed him, and then fatally shot him with his own service revolver. He was captured immediately and given a two life sentences for the killing, a crime that would have earned the death penalty had it been in effect at the time. After being apprehended, Tison told his captors, "I was pretty sure I hit him in the heart so I just went ahead and put two more into him."

In prison, Tison was the only inmate allowed to wear cowboy boots. He convinced the guards that it was necessary because of a bad ankle. He was also regarded as a sort of celebrity by the other prisoners, and it was that adulation that drew Randy Greenawalt's attention. Although Greenawalt was much younger than Tison, he was just as cold-blooded. They became cellmates and behaved themselves well enough to secure quarters in the minimum-security ward.

History would later record that security at the prison was lax, and that both Tison and Greenawalt were given special privileges because Tison had allegedly been involved in the murder of a prisoner whose testimony might have incriminated certain prison officials.

The snitch's name was Tony Serra. He had allegedly told a Phoenix attorney about possible corruption in the prison over land fraud convictions. Four other inmates attacked him, stabbed him fifteen times and battered his head with steel pipes. They tore one ear almost completely off, then held him down and smashed his head with an electric drill. To make sure he was dead, they punched a hole in his head with a drill bit.

Tison was suspected but never indicted. But he allegedly told others that he had been offered fifty thousand dollars to get rid of "a dude in the land fraud." About the same time, he wrote to relatives that he was anticipating an escape that would not only be successful, but also let him flee to Central America where he planned to negotiate a movie contract for a script he figured he could sell to Hollywood.

The prison's lackadaisical visitation rules would be a major asset. Family members were allowed to enter the yards without being screened, patted down, or otherwise checked. That would play a major role in what happened on the morning of July 30, 1978.

Tison's son Raymond entered the visitation area that day for what appeared to be a routine visit. He and his brothers, Ricky and Donald, frequently drove to Florence from Casa Grande to visit their father, and they were known as good boys who could "get along with anyone and everyone." Ricky and Donald arrived about the same time, carrying a large ice chest which they said was loaded with food for a family picnic. But the chest actually contained three sawed-off shotguns and two changes of clothing.

As one of the guards approached and said he was going to open the chest, Ricky pulled out one of the shotguns and aimed it at the man's head. For the next twenty minutes, the four Tisons and Greenawalt put their plan into action. Greenawalt disabled the prison alarm system, and then helped the Tisons round up seven guards and lock them in a storage closet. Then the two inmates put on the street clothes and walked nonchalantly out of the prison entrance. One of the sons was swinging the keys to the family's Ford Galaxy that sat waiting for them in the parking lot. A tower guard watched them depart, totally unaware of what was happening.

Gary Tison had help from his three sons
when he escaped from prison.
ARIZONA DEPARTMENT OF CORRECTIONS

Or what would happen next.

After leaving the prison area, the escapees and the Tison sons abandoned the Ford and proceeded to an isolated house where the brothers had parked a Lincoln Continental. But the car had a flat tire, so they were forced to change it, leaving them without a spare. They spent two nights at the house, and then used the back roads and secondary highways to make their way toward the California border while a statewide manhunt was being organized. The rugged landscape was hard on the Lincoln, and it suffered a blowout near Quartzsite. With no spare available, the group decided to drive slowly to a main highway to flag down a passing car.

Raymond Tison acted the part of the stranded motorist by standing in front of the Lincoln, while the other four hid by the side of the road. One car passed without slowing down. The second, a Mazda occupied by Marine Sergeant John Lyons, his wife Donnelda, his two-year-old son Christopher, and his fifteen-year-old niece Theresa Tyson, pulled up. They were on their way to San Diego, where Lyons was stationed. The Marine got out and offered to help. As Ray showed him the flat tire, the other Tisons and Greenawalt arose from their hiding place and pointed their shotguns at the unfortunate family.

The gunmen forced their captives into the back seat of the Lincoln. Gary Tison ordered Raymond and Donald to drive the partially disabled car down a dirt road off the main highway, then down a gas-line service road farther out into the desert. The other three followed in the confiscated Mazda. When they stopped, the fugitives parked the cars trunk to trunk and the Lyons family was forced to stand in front of the Lincoln's headlights. While the Tison gang was transferring their belongings into the Mazda, they found the family's guns and money, which they kept on the assumption that both would assist them in their escape.

Once the transfer was complete, Gary Tison told Raymond to drive the Lincoln and the hostages farther into the desert. Gary and the others followed, and when the Lincoln stopped, he got out and fired a blast from his shotgun into the radiator to make sure it was totally disabled. Then he ordered the family to stand in front of the car while he pointed the gun at them. Lyons pleaded for mercy. "Jesus, don't kill us," he begged. Gary Tison responded that he "was thinking about it." Next, Lyons asked for water and Gary sent his sons back to the other car to get some. While describing the situation later, Raymond said his father "was like in conflict with himself . . . What it was, I think it was the baby being there and all this, and he wasn't sure about what to do."

Gary and Greenawalt held their guns on the family while the brothers filled the water jug and took it back to their father. He and Greenawalt then went behind the Lincoln and began firing. Lyons, his wife and the toddler died instantly. Mortally wounded, Theresa Tyson was left to die on the desert floor. She managed to crawl away from the bloodbath, but died from her injuries and exposure. Gary Tison told his sons that the four had to be killed because, if left alive, they could tell authorities where the gang was headed and describe the Mazda.

Less than a week later, authorities got what they presumed was a break when Gary Tison called his brother, Joe, in Casa Grande. Although the brother had changed the spelling of his last name to Tyson to distance himself from Gary and his sons, he was nonetheless suspected with being involved in the prison escape. So authorities tapped his phone and waited for the call that they figured was inevitable. When it came, Gary asked his brother to meet him at a small airport in eastern New Mexico and help make arrangements to fly the gang out of the country. Joe said he'd be there, but only because he had agreed to cooperate with the law enforcement agents working the case, in an effort to lessen the consequences he faced.

Joe Tyson, accompanied by Pinal County Sheriff Sergeant Dave Harrington, traveled to an air strip outside of Clovis, New Mexico. They arrived on August 6, but were met by television crews, not the Tison gang. There had been a leak; the Tisons and Greenawalt were long gone. Harrington later told a newspaper reporter that the leak, in his opinion, was directly responsible for two more deaths.

Days later, the escapees drove to the Four Corners area where, police believe, they murdered newlyweds James and Margene Judge in the same brutal fashion as the Lyons family. The Amarillo, Texas, couple was honeymooning in southwestern Colorado. They had been shot to death and dumped in a remote campground near Pagosa Springs. Their bodies were not discovered until November. The killers also stole the couple's Ford Econoline van.

Although the gang had traveled hundreds of miles in a figure eight pattern across Arizona and New Mexico, Pinal County authorities were certain they would eventually return to Tison's home area. "There was no doubt they were going to come back to Pinal County," Harrington said. "Every time he [Gary] escaped, he always ended back in Casa Grande."

The sheriff was right.

On the evening of August 10, a Border Patrol armory at Gila Bend was burglarized. When notified of the break-in, Pinal County Sheriff Frank Reyes called for roadblocks on two roads near Casa Grande. Then Department of Highway Safety authorities learned the gang hadn't been responsible for the burglary and called off the roadblocks. But the word never got to the sheriff's deputies, so they stayed.

Around two o'clock in the morning, the van roared through the first roadblock. "I'll always remember the time," Harrington said. "I'll always remember the time. It was 2:02 a.m."

Donald Tison was driving while his father and Greenawalt fired at the officers. Nobody got hit. Harrington was stationed at the second roadblock about five miles away. He and his men got immediate word that the van was headed their way. Moments later, it appeared, headlights piercing the dark as it roared toward them. The lawman opened fire.

"We weren't shooting at the tires," Harrington recalled. "We were shooting at the vehicle—shooting to hit anything we could." During the gunfight, a bullet fired by one of the four officers at the roadblock hit Donald Tison and the van skidded off the road. Gary Tison leaped from the vehicle and yelled, "Every man for himself!" He then fled into the desert. When the shooting stopped, the officers crawled to the van and found Donald taking his last breaths. Raymond and Ricky Tison and Greenawalt fled, but were apprehended immediately and returned to prison.

More than three hundred police officers and hundreds of volunteers searched for Gary Tison without success. But he couldn't elude the Sonoran Desert. He died of exposure in the blistering heat. His body was found eleven days after the shootout, bloated and desiccated and partially eaten by insects.

The *Casa Grande Dispatch* ran a full page photo of his corpse, blackened and curled under the flimsy shade of a palo verde tree.

Back at the prison, Raymond Tison told authorities where to find the Lincoln containing the bodies of the Lyons family. Lyons was lying near the car with close-range gunshot wounds to his head, shoulders, chest, and wrists. The body of his twenty-three-year-old wife was in the back seat, cradling the baby. She had been shot in the chest and neck; the toddler died from a shotgun blast to the head.

The body of Lyons's niece was found about a quarter of a mile away. A bullet had shattered her thigh. Bone fragments that pierced her abdomen caused her to bleed to death. Officers found a leather dog collar buckled around her ankle. Apparently she had tried to stop the bleeding. The dog's body was found next to hers.

When Greenawalt arrived back at the prison, he was placed in the back of a pickup truck where he was strip-searched, then questioned. The interrogation ended when he asked for an attorney, but a second group of police officers continued the questioning, a factor that would later lead to an appeal.

Greenawalt and the surviving Tison brothers were charged with ninety-two crimes, including four counts of murder, armed robbery, kidnapping and car theft. (No charges were ever brought for the deaths of the newlywed Judges, and Colorado authorities closed the cases when the others resulted in convictions in Arizona.) They were initially tried together and prosecutors offered a slight degree of leniency if they would provide names of others who assisted in the escape. After they refused, they were then tried individually. Each drew a death sentence.

The state also charged Dorothy Tison in connection with the escape. She pleaded *nolo contendere* to conspiracy and served a nine-month prison term.

The brothers appealed their sentences on the grounds that they were merely accomplices, not murderers. The appeal got all the way to the US Supreme Court, where it was denied by a five-to-four vote. Justice Sandra Day O'Connor wrote, in the majority court opinion:

> *Raymond Tison brought an arsenal of lethal weapons into the Arizona State Prison which he then handed over to two convicted murderers, one of whom he knew had killed a prison guard in the course of a previous escape attempt. By his own admission, he was prepared to kill in furtherance of the prison break. He performed the crucial role of flagging down a passing car occupied by an innocent family whose fate was then entrusted to the known killer he had previously armed. He robbed these people at their direction and then guarded the victims at gunpoint while they considered what next to do. He stood by and watched the killing, making no effort to assist the victims, before, during or after the shooting. Instead, he chose to assist the killers in their continuing criminal endeavors . . .*

The ruling continued:

> *Ricky Tison's behavior differs in slight details only. Like Raymond, he intentionally brought the guns into the prison to arm the murderers. He could have foreseen that lethal force might be used, particularly since he knew that his father's previous escape attempt had resulted in murder. He, too, participated fully in the kidnapping and robbery*

and watched the killing after which he chose to aid those whom he had placed in the position to kill, rather than their victims . . .

These facts not only indicate that the Tison brothers' participation in the crime was anything but minor; they also would clearly support a finding that they both subjectively appreciated that their acts were likely to result in the taking of innocent life . . .

Justice O'Connor concluded that the death penalty would be appropriate for a murder like those committed by the gang if it could be shown that the defendants were major participants.

In 1992, the Arizona Supreme Court ruled the prosecution had failed to prove the brothers had shown reckless indifference toward human life, since their father and Greenawalt had done the actual shootings. Another factor was that both were under twenty years of age when the crimes were committed. Ricky was eighteen; Raymond nineteen. Their death sentences were reduced to life imprisonment.

Greenawalt also used the appeals process to delay the imposition of the death penalty, and it kept him alive for almost twenty years. He had been brought to trial on February 6, 1979, convicted on February 9 and sentenced to death on March 26. Arizona Attorney General Bob Corbin summed it up with:

He deserves it. I hope to hell they carry it out this time. If they'd executed him for his crime the first time, those people might still be alive today.

The appeals contended that Greenawalt had been denied his Fourth and Fifth Amendment rights while being questioned. Every appeal was denied.

And on January 23, 1997, Greenawalt ate a last meal of a cheeseburger and fries, and then was led to the execution chamber. A short time later, it was over.

The episode is still considered one of Arizona's darkest times and led to a major shakeup in the state's prison system. In 1983, it became the subject of a made-for-television movie entitled *A Killer in the Family*. Robert Mitchum portrayed Gary Tison and Stuart Margolin appeared as Randy Greenawalt. It was not well received. The critic for the *New York Times* openly wondered why anyone would be interested in such lowlifes.

The prison at Florence still contains the state's death chamber. Super-strict security measures have been in place since the Tison escapade, but every now and then, somebody makes a run for it. Almost every one has been recaptured.

The exterior looks about the same as it did back when Gary Tison and Randy Greenawalt spent their days and nights there. It was built by inmates and opened in 1908 to replace the old Territorial Prison in Yuma. The convicts were housed in tents during construction. The new facility came equipped with a death chamber, which consisted of scaffolding above the death row cells with a trap door that opened into a room below. Hanging was replaced by the gas chamber as a form of execution in 1933. Now it's lethal injection. More than eighty inmates have met their deaths by one of those forms since the penitentiary opened.

Starting around the turn of the twenty-first century, the city of Florence underwent a minor population explosion, and currently is home to more than twenty-five thousand residents, as well as more than three thousand inmates. Founded in 1866 by Colonel Levi Ruggles, an Indian agent, it is today regarded as a National Historic District due to its high number of fine old buildings. The city's architecture incorporates both rustic adobe brick buildings and more modern structures. Some of the adobes date back to 1868. The most noticeable building is the 1891 Pinal County Courthouse, an excellent example of American Victorian architecture.

Drawing less attention is the Prison Arts Store and Trade Center, a converted mobile home located a short distance west of the prison gates. Everything for sale in the store is made by inmates, either at the Florence prison or other lockups around the state. Goods vary, but usually include wallets, crocheted hats, jewelry, wood carvings, oil paintings, watercolors, and, fittingly, novelty license plates.

CHAPTER TWELVE

Shady Ladies:
Some of Those Womenfolk Weren't Very Nice

L ike most everywhere else, the skeletons in the closets of Arizona's history weren't always those of bad men. There were quite a few women whose deeds (or misdeeds) gained them varying degrees of fame (or infamy).

Three of the more notorious were Eva Dugan, Gabrielle Darley, and Mary Katherine Haroney.

Mary Katherine Haroney?

Try Big Nose Kate.

Eva Dugan was perhaps the worst, and she paid the highest penalty for her crimes. She killed a man and suffered a highly publicized and gruesome death because of it. Her demise also brought about a major change in Arizona's justice system.

She was the only woman ever executed in the state, and one of the last women to die on the gallows in the United States. She was hanged on March 2, 1930, for a murder she had committed three years earlier.

Dugan led the proverbial hard life. She was born in Alaska in 1876 and grew up there during the Yukon Gold Rush. She married when she was only sixteen and bore two children before her husband abandoned her. To support herself and the kids, she worked as a cabaret singer in Juneau, and when that didn't pay enough, she turned to prostitution. Her whereabouts and family life between the time she left Alaska to the time she made her way to Arizona in the mid-1920s are unknown. Her daughter wrote her a letter while Eva was in prison awaiting execution; there is no mention of what happened to the other child.

Convicted murderess Eva Dugan met a horrible fate at the gallows.
SCOTTSDALE CC SOUTHWEST STUDIES

By January 1927, Dugan was working as a housekeeper for Andrew J. Mathis, a wealthy Tucson rancher known as a recluse with a cranky attitude. They did not have a good relationship. He accused her of trying to poison him; she called him cheap and demanding. Two months after hiring her, Mathis fired her and told her to leave his ranch and never return.

A few days afterwards, Mathis was reported missing. Then neighbors became suspicious when Dugan tried to sell them some of her ex-employer's livestock. Their suspicions grew when she claimed Mathis had moved to California and left her all his property. They knew Mathis was tight-fisted, the type of man who would never have willingly given anything away, especially to the woman he had recently dismissed.

Dugan left the area in a hurry, driving her former boss's car. Weeks later, local authorities searched the ranch but didn't find a body. They did, however, find clues that led them to believe Mathis had not left his property voluntarily. Dugan sold the car in Kansas City, Missouri, for $600. She told the dealer she was Mathis's wife and needed the money for his medical bills. In the meantime, authorities had issued a nationwide search for her as a murder suspect. Dugan was arrested in White Plains, New York, when a postal worker intercepted a card she had sent to her father in California. She was extradited to Arizona, but since no one had ever found her ex-employer's body, she was convicted of car theft and sentenced to three years in the state prison at Florence.

But nearly a year later, a camper uncovered a skeleton in a shallow grave dug into the desert outside Tucson. It didn't take long for authorities to determine it was Mathis. They immediately began questioning Eva Dugan; she immediately denied everything. If she had killed the man, she said, she would have buried him so deep the remains would never have been found. But under further interrogation, she changed her story and involved a man she knew only as "Jack." They met at a restaurant, she said, while he was looking for work. She recommended the ranch where she was employed. He went and was hired on the spot, but when Mathis realized that he wasn't cut out to be a ranch hand, they got into an argument that ended when Jack hit Mathis with such force that it killed him.

Dugan said she wanted to go for help but Jack said if she didn't help dispose of the body, he'd leave and she'd be accused of murder. So she helped. At least, that's what she told authorities.

Under scrutiny, her story didn't hold up. She was charged with murder. During the trial, her lawyers tried an insanity plea and called doctors who testified that her mental state might have been compromised because she had syphilis. It didn't work. A jury convicted her of first-degree murder and a judge sentenced her to death by hanging. As she was being escorted from the courtroom after hearing the verdict, Eva said bitterly, "Well, I guess you're satisfied now."

She was returned to her cell in Florence, where precautions were taken to make sure she didn't cheat the noose by committing suicide. The warden ordered all pieces of glass, metal, and wood removed from the entire cell block. Her lawyers went through the appeals process but lost every one. For more than two years, her supporters tried to have the death sentence commuted. They failed on every attempt.

Distraught and resigned, she told her jailers that she didn't want to be buried in the prison cemetery; they provided her with the small tools necessary to create embroidered items she could sell to raise money for a proper burial. They allowed her to grant interviews for one dollar each. She wrote to her father in California, asking him for financial help. He sent fifty dollars. Her cellmates each chipped in fifty cents toward the purchase of the fancy coffin she wanted rather than the no-frills wooden box provided by the prison.

As her execution date neared, Dugan sewed her own silk burial dress and earned enough to pay for a decent burial. On the day before she was to hang, prison officials heard a rumor that she was going to kill herself, so they searched her cell and found a vial of raw ammonia and several razor blades hidden in her dress. She said they were for medicinal purposes, and that she was willing to let the law take its course. She visited with friends and joked with the guards. She told a newspaper reporter, "I am going to my maker with a clear conscience."

When the guards told her that the hanging might ruin her silk dress, she agreed to wear prison garb up the steps to the gallows, but asked that she be buried in the dress. She played cards all night, bantered with newsmen and posed for photographs. She read a telegram from her daughter, who said she was praying for her and told her to be brave. She cried when she was told that her eighty-two-year-old father could not come to see her. When a friend said someone had ordered cut flowers for her funeral, she replied, "I don't want that. I like to see flowers growing, but cut flowers have always been my jinx."

Her evening meal was a large bowl of oyster stew, which she cooked herself. The next morning, her final meal of steak and lamb chops was left untouched. Prison officials said they had never seen anyone so calm while awaiting certain death.

As the warden and guards escorted her to the gallows, she sang something about, "I don't know where I'm going but I'm on my way." Then she walked resolutely up the thirteen steps. Asked if she had any last words, she remained silent. One of her guards spoke. "She has nothing to say," he said. The trap beneath her was sprung at 5:01 a.m. As she plummeted to her death, her head was jerked from her body and rolled toward the sixty spectators who had gathered to witness the execution. It was the first time women had been allowed to view a legal hanging. Two of them fainted. The others fled, ashen-faced and gasping.

Despite her wishes to be buried elsewhere, Eva Dugan's body was interred in the small plot behind the prison. Within days, Arizona lawmakers enacted legislation that replaced the noose with the gas chamber.

Today, one exhibit in the Pinal County Historical Museum in Florence draws particular attention. It's called the Arizona State Prison Collection, and what they have collected are the nooses involved in the executions of convicted murderers at the nearby prison. There are twenty-eight nooses on display. The seventeenth noose was used to hang Eva Dugan.

Gabrielle Darley also killed a man—maybe more than one. But even though she openly admitted her crime, she was never convicted and never faced the executioner.

Her life story was filled with the traumas brought on by the hardships of turn-of-the-twentieth-century life. She was born in France in 1890, and her mother left for America with her daughter but without her husband around 1900. They settled in San Francisco, where her mother died in the 1906 earthquake. Left without parents at age sixteen, Darley wandered into the gold fields of Nevada and tried to eke out a living as a waitress. The easy spending habits of the miners convinced her there were other sources of income, so she became a prostitute.

Young, pretty, and skilled, she did well in the profession. She bought fancy jewels and planned to open a brothel. But first, she married Ernest Presti, an Italian gambler and boxer who fought under the name of Kid Kirby. They moved to Prescott where she opened her own house of ill repute and both plied their respective trades. Gabrielle was a much better madam than her husband was a boxer. He lost almost every bout, and then gambled away a lot of his wife's money at the dice and poker tables. Both forms of loss came to an abrupt end in May 1911, when Presti was shot and killed by a shoeshine man over a $20 gambling debt. Talk around Prescott was that Gabrielle had a good reason to have him killed. She was never charged, but the episode cast a cloud of suspicion that would follow her for the rest of her life.

Then she met Leonard Topp, the man who would become her client, then her lover, and then her victim.

Topp frequented her establishment and eventually became Gabrielle's regular companion. But he ended their relationship when he ran away with one of Gabrielle's working girls. That was bad enough, but he also absconded with a substantial portion of Gabrielle's diamond jewelry and cash. It wasn't his smartest move. And he would pay the full penalty for it.

Darley hired a private detective to track him down. He found Topp and his new girlfriend in Los Angeles; Gabrielle took one of the next trains out of Prescott. There are at least two versions of what happened when the two met again. According to one account, she encountered him in a jewelry store where he was using the stolen money to buy a diamond ring for his new lady friend. The other account places their final meeting in a liquor store that Topp had purchased with his ex-girlfriend's money. But both accounts share the same ending: Topp was about to die.

Gabrielle Darley did not have good relationships with men.
PHOTO COURTESY OF SHARLOT HALL MUSEUM LIBRARY AND ARCHIVES, PRESCOTT, ARIZONA

According to an eyewitness, Gabrielle walked in and hissed, "Hello, Leonard." He turned to face her; she withdrew the pistol she had concealed in her fur muff and fired a single shot. Her aim was deadly. The bullet hit Topp's heart, but he lived long enough to knock Darley down and smash her head against the floor, knocking her unconscious. He then stood up and said, "Well, I guess I'm about through for good," and fell over dead.

Gabrielle Darley was arrested and charged with murder.

Her trial became front-page news all across the country. Major newspapers sent their best reporters to Los Angeles to cover the event, and their stories were published under headlines that screamed "She Did It Because She Loved Him." Their coverage frequently replaced World War I reports as the lead stories. Some likened her to "Frankie," the wronged woman in the popular ballad "Frankie and Johnny." One of her working girls testified that Topp had abused Gabrielle by kicking her while wearing heavy boots.

A contrite Darley appeared in court every day, wearing the countenance of a helpless woman who had been victimized by a brutal man. One reporter said she "gave the jury her best impression of a lost soul adrift in a heartless world." She must have been exceptionally convincing because an all-male jury found her not guilty after deliberating for only eight minutes. Adela Rogers St. John, a reporter who covered the case, wrote that with men like Topp, "Homicide is not only justifiable, but obligatory."

The incident didn't end there, however. It became the subject of a movie entitled *The Red Kimono,* released in 1928. Unaware of the content, Darley went to see it one night in Prescott, and was outraged when she realized she was the woman depicted on the screen. The moviemakers even used her full name. She filed a $50,000 lawsuit against the producer, Dorothy Reid, for invasion of privacy, claiming that although she did shoot and kill Topp, she was acquitted and had returned to Prescott and become a respected citizen. But by using her real name, she claimed, the movie depicted her as "a woman of lewd character, a prostitute and a murderer."

The courts upheld her suit and expressed outrage over the producer's lack of judgment. The ruling said, "It was wrong to destroy Gabrielle's reputation, wrong to injure her standing in society by publishing the story of her former life for the sole purpose of making money." Reid appealed to the California Supreme Court but that body refused to hear the case.

But, despite her testimony that she was now a model citizen, Darley did not give up her activities as a seller of sin. She returned to Prescott and resumed her role as a madam, operating out of several downtown hotels along the city's infamous Whiskey Row. She was accepted, but not respected. Her contemporaries said she was a "pretty, but plump woman" who took good care of her employees.

She also found time to get remarried. This time, it was to Bernard Melvin. He also had sticky fingers, and that ended the marriage after only six months. He dug into Gabrielle's bank account and left town. She followed him to California, and had him arrested on the grounds that he had embezzled $2,000 from her establishment. When the Los Angeles press heard about it, they remembered her trial and jumped all over the story. She refused their requests for interviews, but Melvin was more than willing to give his side. "I didn't steal any money from her," he told the *Los Angeles Times*. "She gave it to me. We loved each other once, but we're through now and she hates me. She hated Topp and she killed him. I'm in jail. The man always pays, I guess."

Melvin was convicted and sentenced to prison time. After his release, he returned to Prescott and became a caretaker at the town dump. In 1927, he was beaten and robbed and died as a result of his injuries in 1929.

So Gabrielle's scorecard now read: THREE MEN IN HER LIFE. THREE DEATHS.

But she still wasn't done strolling down the aisle. Shortly after Melvin's death, she married Everett Fretz, a barber. It was another short-lived union. Fretz had mental problems, and they worsened after the marriage. He raved about an imaginary gold mine and said people were out to steal it from him. He demanded that the local sheriff deputize him so he could protect the alleged treasure. His ranting became so bad that his wife had him committed to the Arizona State Asylum in 1935. He died a short time later at age forty. The medical staff said his symptoms were similar to those caused by ingesting poison, but ruled that the death was the result of "general paralysis of the insane."

Four men.

Four deaths.

The inference that poison might have been the cause of death popped up again later, after Gabrielle married George Wiley. She was getting older and the hard life was taking its toll. She was no longer young and pretty; by now she was dowdy and frowsy. But Wiley wasn't much of a catch, either. He was short, overweight, and red-faced. And so they wed.

They left Prescott to operate a combination liquor store, cafe, auto court and gas station they had purchased in nearby Salome. Gabrielle began calling herself "Dollie" and life went on as before. She even brought some of her girls along with her and provided them with working quarters in cabins behind the store.

But death and Dollie weren't done with each other.

In late 1940, Wiley and Mae Grissom, one of Dollie's working girls, got into an argument that led to a physical confrontation. When Wiley lunged at the girl, she fell backward and hit her head on a water cooler. Her injuries were so severe that she was taken to a hospital in Wickenburg, where she died two weeks later, shortly after Dollie had paid her a visit.

Wiley was charged with murder in connection with the death, but he never made it to trial. On January 10, 1941, he was found dead in his home. Authorities said he had taken a drink from a glass that contained rat poison. The rumors started immediately.

Five men.

Five deaths.

A coroner's inquest was called because there were suspicions that Dollie had deliberately left the poisoned glass on the counter where her husband was sure to find it. There were also insinuations that maybe Mae Grissom hadn't died from her head injury, but possibly from poison. But the coroner's jury ignored speculation and ruled that the girl had died of natural causes and that Wiley's death was suicide.

Gabrielle "Dollie" Darley Presti Melvin Fretz Wiley died in a Wickenburg hospital on Christmas Day, 1962, at age seventy-two. Her body was cremated and the ashes interred next to the grave of Everett Fretz.

Although Mary Katharine Haroney went by many names during her life, history favors "Big Nose Kate," despite the lack of a plausible explanation for the name. Two theories, however, seem to have the most credibility. One theory is that she actually did have a rather large nose. The second theory is that she was known for sticking her rather large nose into other folks' business.

And, although she led a vigorous life filled with many adventures, she is best remembered for her extended, but stormy, relationship with John Henry "Doc" Holliday, one of the participants in the infamous gunfight at the OK Corral in Tombstone. She once saved him from a lynch mob and, according to some historians, she was with him when he died.

Her march into history began on November 7, 1850, in Budapest, Hungary, when she was born to the union of Dr. Michael Haroney and his second wife, Katharina Baldizar Haroney. Her family was wealthy and well-accepted in society, so she received an education befitting her status, becoming fluent in Hungarian, French, Spanish, and English. Her family left Europe and moved to Mexico City in 1862 when Dr. Haroney was appointed the personal physician to Emperor Maximilian I, the ruler of French-controlled Mexico. In 1865, when the revolution against Maximilian began, the family relocated to Iowa.

Following the deaths of both parents that year, Mary Katharine and five of her siblings were placed in foster care. When she was sixteen, she ran away from her new home and stowed away on a Mississippi River steamboat bound for St. Louis, Missouri. The captain discovered her but let her stay on the boat until it

Mary Katherine Harony was better known as Big Nose Kate.
SCOTTSDALE CC SOUTHWEST STUDIES

reached St. Louis, where he helped her financially and enrolled her in school. In gratitude, Kate took his last name of Fisher. She stayed in Missouri and before her twentieth birthday, she became a wife, mother, and widow. She married Silas Melvin and had a baby, but both her husband and their child died in the same year.

Details of her whereabouts for the next few years are sketchy, but by 1874 she was in Dodge City, Kansas, working as a dance hall girl under the name of Kate Elder. Later, she allegedly found employment as a "sporting girl" in an establishment operated by Nellie Bessie Earp, wife of James Earp, oldest of the Earp brothers. In her last years, she would deny that she was ever a prostitute. However, historians insist that she was, and that she stayed with it after meeting Holliday. Frequently, they maintain, her earnings provided Holliday with his gambling money. What is certain is that she met Holliday around that time, either in Dodge City or Fort Griffin, Texas.

Although a licensed dentist, Holliday had pretty much given up his practice and was making his living as a gambler in several towns after their relationship began. His relationship with Kate was rocky from the start because they both were stubborn and had violent tempers. Together, they plied their respective trades across Colorado and New Mexico and as far north as South Dakota. Kate proved to be a valuable consort. She proved her worth one night in 1877, when Holliday got into a fight with Ed Bailey during a game of chance in Fort Griffin.

Bailey was known as a bully who cheated at cards. Holliday accused him of looking at discards, a practice strictly prohibited in poker. The accusations led to harsh words. Bailey pulled a gun but before he could shoot, Holliday slashed him across the midsection with a knife. The bully died within minutes and Holliday was arrested and confined to a room in a hotel because the town didn't have a jail. Even though he had acted in self-defense, the townspeople took umbrage at the death of one of their own, and a hastily organized vigilante group made its way toward the hotel.

Big Nose Kate acted immediately. She set fire to a shed near the hotel and it was quickly engulfed in flames. As the fire spread, the vigilante group decided it was better to save their town than hang a gambler, so they gave up their initial quest and started dousing the blaze. While that was going on, Kate stuck a gun in the guard's face, disarmed him, and released Holliday. They fled from the hotel, hid out overnight, then stole horses and made their way to Dodge City.

Once in Dodge, they parted company. Holliday left for Colorado and wound up in Las Vegas, New Mexico, where he got into another deadly saloon confrontation, this time with Mike Gordon, another blowhard. Doc was part owner of the saloon and ordered Gordon out after he made threats against one of the barmaids. They argued; Gordon wound up dead from a bullet wound. The lynch mob formed; Holliday left town before they got to him. He fled back to Dodge City, and then headed into Arizona Territory.

The two ran into each other in Prescott. Doc was on a winning streak and Kate was willing to keep him company, both at the tables and later in his hotel room. In the summer of 1880, they reached Tombstone. He stayed; she went to Globe and opened a boarding house, which many said was actually a brothel. Holliday visited often, and she took time off to travel to Tombstone to see him. But by this time, Kate's temper and drinking were becoming a problem. She became abusive toward Holliday and he ended the relationship. It was an almost fatal decision on his part.

In mid-March 1881, four masked men held up a stagecoach east of Tombstone and killed the driver and a passenger. Holliday was accused of being involved and when Sheriff Johnny Behan found Kate in a drunken stupor, he fed her more whiskey and coerced her into signing an affidavit that said Doc was one of the masked robbers. When she sobered up, she realized what she'd done and immediately retracted her statement, so the charge against Holliday was thrown out.

But the relationship was definitely over this time. Holliday gave Kate some money, put her on a stagecoach and told her never to return. However, toward the end of her life, she claimed she was in a hotel in Tombstone on Oct. 26, 1881, the day of the historic shootout. She told a reporter that she witnessed the fight and afterward, she went to Holliday's room and bandaged the wound in his side. She claimed Holliday wept and said, "It was awful. It was awful." However, she was eighty-nine years old when she told the story so there was speculation that her memory may have been failing, casting doubt on the account. According to legend, Kate was with Holliday in Colorado when he died of tuberculosis in 1887.

After Holliday's death, she met and married George Cummings in 1888 and they returned to Arizona. The marriage lasted only a year because he was an abusive alcoholic. Kate found work as a hotel maid in Cochise, then moved in with John Howard and stayed with him until his death in 1930. In 1931, at age eighty-one, she petitioned the state for admission to the Arizona Pioneers Home in Prescott. Her request was initially denied because she had never become an American citizen, but was granted six months later and she became one of the first female residents.

She died there on November 2, 1940, and was buried under the name of Mary K. Cummings.

CHAPTER THIRTEEN
John Shaw:
A Stiff Drink for a Stiff

It wasn't so much what John Shaw did during his brief lifetime that earned him a cameo role in the drama of the Old West. What happened after his violent death, however, definitely made his name worth mentioning.

Like many of his peers, Shaw was killed during a shootout with lawmen and was ignominiously buried in one of the many boot hills that sprang up on the Western frontier when there were more dead bodies than undertakers. But his story had an unusual twist at the end, the result of a peculiar cowboy code of honor—and too much whiskey.

Shaw was young, perhaps twenty-four or twenty-five, when the incident that launched him into infamy began. He was but a couple of days older when it ended. Over that short span, he went from unfortunate holdup man to curious legend. He was there when it all played out, but he was an active participant only in the first part.

On the night of April 5, 1905, two strangers took part in the familiar scenario of stopping in for a drink. One was tall, one was short. The town was Winslow, Arizona Territory, and the bar was the Wigwam Saloon. The two ordered shots of whiskey and paid for them, but left the filled glasses sitting on the bar while they turned to watch the action taking place before them. The Wigwam was also a gambling hall so it was filled with card players and dice rollers, most of them losing their money in the customary ways.

One table in particular drew the interest of the two newcomers because it was covered with stacks of silver dollars, worth between $300 and $500. The pair hesitated momentarily before one drew his gun and ordered everyone in the place to stay calm to avoid unnecessary gunfire while he and his companion removed the silver dollars from the table and stuffed them into their pockets. Once they had grabbed as many coins as they could carry, they hustled out of the bar without taking anything from any of the other patrons. They also left the two full glasses of whiskey on the bar.

Although Winslow was known as a rough and rather lawless settlement, such a brazen holdup took the victims by surprise. They just sat there for as long as ten minutes before anyone took action. The delay may have been due to the fact that some of the gamblers were members of the notorious Hashknife Outfit and were probably playing with money they had stolen from someone else. That might be hard to explain if the law started snooping around. Eventually, however, they contacted Deputy Sheriff J. C. "Pete" Pemberton and Marshal Bob Giles to report their ill fortune.

The next afternoon, *The Winslow Mail* reported that the incident had occurred at about 1:30 a.m., and noted that the pair got away with an estimated $250. The story also said that somebody in the saloon fired up to three shots at the robbers but didn't hit either one.

"This is about the boldest robbery that has occurred in this city in a long while," the report declared. "It will probably be a hard job to apprehend the men, but we believe they will be caught and brought to do time before long, as our officers have some good clues."

The lawmen had started the search immediately, but the "good clues" consisted of some boot tracks and a trail of seven silver dollars leading up to the nearby railroad tracks. They guessed the robbers had boarded a train and headed west. After being notified by telegraph, Navajo County Sheriff C. I. "Chet" Houck left his office in Holbrook to join Pemberton, and the two lawmen climbed aboard the next train for Flagstaff, about forty-five miles to the west. Both men were handy with a gun. Houck had a reputation as a no-nonsense sheriff who hanged men first and asked questions later. Pemberton was a Texas gunslinger who came to Arizona as a participant in the Pleasant Valley Range War and later worked for the Hashknife Outfit.

The trip to Flagstaff was futile; nobody there had seen the flee-ing duo so the officers climbed on an eastbound train that would take them back to Winslow. Then their luck changed.

As the train passed Canyon Diablo, a seedy railroad encamp-ment about halfway between Flagstaff and Winslow, a brakeman and conductor overheard Houck and Pemberton discussing the case and said they had seen two suspicious-looking men lurking in the brush along the railroad right-of-way at the canyon. The lawmen stopped the train and decided to walk back to town. It was late evening when they got there.

Canyon Diablo was a miserable place. More of a chasm than an actual canyon, it was about 225 feet deep but more than five hundred feet wide. Its configuration resisted any attempt to make a road across it, so the westbound wagon trains had to detour to the north, across the Little Colorado River, or far to the south.

The deep gorge was used by Apache raiders as a hiding place after they raided Navajo encampments. The Apaches would steal horses and women and escape into the canyon. When the Navajos went after them, they vanished into the side canyons and caves.

According to one historical account, Navajo scouts found an Apache party inside one of the caves and took drastic action. They gathered a large amount of sagebrush, set the pile on fire and shoved it into the mouth of the cave. The next morning, so the story goes, the Navajos discovered forty-two charred bodies inside.

The history of Canyon Diablo, the town, wasn't much better. From the time it sprang up until its unheralded demise, it was a hellhole, inhabited by an unholy assortment of lowlifes and mis-fits. It had been established around 1880, near a canyon that the Atlantic and Pacific Railroad had to cross to complete its trans-continental line. Construction was halted so the rail workers could build a bridge to span the canyon. Engineering and financial complications delayed the process, so the town of Canyon Diablo erupted to serve the workmen and those who followed: cowboys, prospectors, hunters, sheepherders, pilgrims, and drifters. Almost as soon as the town was established, it was filled with saloons, brothels, gambling halls, and dance halls that doubled as broth-els. They never closed. Shootouts were routine and historians say as many as thirty-five men were gunned down during the town's brief existence. There was little law because few were willing to stand up to the criminal element. One tale says the first sheriff pinned his badge on at 3 p.m., and was shot and killed before sun-set. None of those who followed him in the office lasted more than a month before they were either killed or forced to leave. Local gamblers often made bets on how long the next sheriff would last.

One of the short-term sheriffs was known as Bill Duckin, who lasted longer than most of the others but eventually met the same fate. Duckin purchased a new suit and cut out the pockets of the long coat so he could draw and fire without whipping back the coat-tails. He never finished second in a gunfight until he bought another suit but neglected to remove the pockets. The first time he wore it, he was gunned down by someone with no respect for sartorial trickery.

The lawlessness continued. On March 21, 1889, four bandits held up a train and escaped with a substantial amount of cash and jewelry. Some put the total at more than $40,000. Yavapai County Sheriff Buckey O'Neill of Prescott arrived in Canyon Diablo with a posse and followed the robbers into Utah, where he caught them after a twenty-three-day chase. They recovered less than one thou-sand dollars, which led to the rumor that most of the loot was buried somewhere in the canyon. According to some legends, it's still there.

O'Neill went on to become mayor of Prescott, and later became famous as a captain of Teddy Roosevelt's Rough Riders in the Spanish-American War. He was killed during a battle at Kettle Hill on July 1, 1898.

The number of men killed in Canyon Diablo's brief existence surpassed the combined death tolls of Tombstone, Dodge City, and Abilene for the same period. And many of them were buried where they fell, if it was convenient. One former resident told a historian, "You just stuck 'em in the ground any old place."

There were some legitimate businesses, such as supply stores and restaurants, but most of the monetary transactions consisted of someone forcibly taking money from someone else. The town's lowlifes rolled drunks in broad daylight, and the bodies of those murdered on the streets were often buried where they fell because there was no cemetery. Eventually, even the hardened residents of Canyon Diablo got tired of that practice so they set aside a small plot of ground for use as a burial ground. But the graves of those who went to their final resting places there were shallow; the ground was too hard and rocky to dig down more than a couple of feet.

Naturally, when the boys showed up, so did the girls. The ladies of the evening were usually employed by the likes of Gotch-eyed Mary, Bigfoot Annie, and California Lil, all skilled in the business of providing female companionship. They were fierce competitors for the ill-gotten dollar. On one occasion, Bigfoot Annie used a sawed-off shotgun to permanently remove Gotch-eyed Mary and two of her employees from circulation.

Later that same night, Annie went to her final destination when someone slashed her throat with a razor. The suspicion was that a gambler friend of one of the victims evened the score, but he was killed the next day so the slaying went unsolved. Holdups and robberies were daily occurrences and anyone with even a small amount of money on his person was a target.

Once the metal span over the canyon was taken over and finished by the Atchison, Topeka and Santa Fe Railroad, the town began to die. But the violence persisted. The "law of the gun" became so bad that those who hadn't deserted the community asked the Army to take over law enforcement. That act, coupled with the completion of the bridge, caused many of the drifters and lawbreakers who had menaced the town for almost two decades to move on. So when Pemberton and Houck arrived on April 6, 1905, Canyon Diablo was a mere shadow of its former self. One of those who stayed was Fred Volz, owner of a trading post. The sheriff and his deputy went immediately to his place and started asking questions. Volz said he'd seen two fugitives, and just as he was giving their descriptions, the suspects came into view, walking along the railroad tracks directly toward the lawmen.

It was about 6:30 p.m. The gathering darkness made it difficult to determine if the two were actually the wanted men so Houck stopped them and asked if they had seen any suspicious characters. They said they hadn't, but the sheriff told them he was going to search them anyway. The tall one stepped back and snarled, "Nobody searches us!" When Houck insisted, the suspects pulled their guns and began firing. There are several accounts of what happened next.

According to the story published in the *Winslow Mail* a week later, after that first bullet tore through the lower half of the sheriff's coat, he pulled out his own six-gun and began shooting. His first lead missile struck the robber in the abdomen but he didn't go down. Instead, he kept firing at Houck until he ran out of bullets. Houck ended the confrontation with a shot through the temple. The man fell and never moved.

While all that was going on, Pemberton and the short man were also blazing away at each other. The robber fired first but only hit the shoulder of the lawman's coat. Pemberton emptied his gun with return gunfire. His first bullet shattered his enemy's left wrist; the next nailed him in the hip. Seemingly aware that he was beaten, the man walked a little distance down the railroad tracks before he sat down and said he'd had enough. But as Houck approached him, the outlaw aimed directly at his head and probably would have killed the sheriff if Pemberton hadn't shown up at the right moment. A split second before the suspect was able to fire, the deputy's last bullet slammed into the man's shoulder and threw his aim off.

It was fortunate for Houck that Pemberton had a bullet left. In those days, most men carried six-guns but the standard load was five bullets because early revolvers had no safety mechanism. If the hammer was over a chamber with a live round and the weapon was dropped or the hammer accidentally struck, it would fire, so loading a sixth missile was considered too risky. But Pemberton carried his revolver with the sixth bullet, and that factor, although probably reckless, saved Houck's life—and ended the shootout.

A total of twenty-one rounds had been fired within a matter of seconds, but even though the combatants stood within six feet of each other, few of their bullets did any damage. The only real casualty was the taller outlaw who lay dead on the ground before them. That prompted questions into how they could miss each other so often at such close range. Eyewitness accounts supported later contentions that the inaccuracies were the result of drawing too fast and shooting too quick, powder flashes from the six-shooters that may have blinded the participants, and shaky hands caused by outright fear.

When things settled down, the lawmen arrested the surviving outlaw, who gave his name as William Smythe. He said the dead man was John Shaw. They found $117.45 on Shaw's body and retrieved another $154 from Smythe. A coroner from Flagstaff conducted an inquest and a hastily assembled jury exonerated the sheriff. Houck got a camera from the trading post and tried to take a photo of the dead man to verify his identity and possibly tie him to other crimes. But it was dark and there was no flash powder. They jury-rigged a flash system using gunpowder from a shotgun shell, but it didn't work. So he and Pemberton acquired a wooden coffin from Volz, put Shaw's body inside and lowered it into the shallow grave they had dug in the community's Boot Hill, a graveyard for men who died violent deaths with their boots still on. Then they took their prisoner back to Winslow where the newspaper account declared that "two desperate characters were brought to justice by two brave and efficient lawmen."

Then the story moved on to its bizarre second ending.

When word of the shootout reached the Wigwam Saloon, the holdup victims rejoiced and celebrated with large amounts of whiskey. And the more whiskey they consumed, the more they developed a strange case of morality. They remembered the booze-filled glasses the robbers had left on the bar and said it wasn't right that they paid for the whiskey and didn't get to drink it. They also expressed an extreme dislike for Sheriff Houck and said it was just like him to bury Shaw without offering a final shot of whiskey.

The exact wording of what transpired next was never written down but one published report said that Sam Case, a member of the Hashknife Outfit, exclaimed, "It just ain't right, him not getting his shot of forty red. We should go down to Canyon Diablo, dig him up, and give him a snort."

So they did.

Intent upon righting what they considered an unprincipled wrong, an odd assortment of cowboys, gamblers, and town drunks—about fifteen in all, with many of them carrying bottles of whiskey—caught a late night train for Canyon Diablo. It was early morning when they arrived. They roused Volz from his bed at the trading post and convinced him to lend them a shovel. They staggered to the graveyard where Shaw's grave was easy to find because it was only a day old. After digging through the loose dirt, they opened the coffin, extricated the body and propped it up against a picket fence surrounding another grave.

Rigor mortis had already set in. The motley crew had to force the jaw partially open to pour whiskey from a long-necked bottle through the clenched teeth. Years later, Lucien Creswell, one of the participants, told author Gladwell Richardson that ". . . something about the way he looked struck home. He might have been any of us, a saddle pard, a brother. There are some who called us grave robbers, ghouls for digging him up. But then and there it seemed to us that getting him a final drink was right and proper *salud* to a man who, when he went under, went down fighting."

Volz lent them a box camera, the same one the sheriff tried to use, and suggested that they take photographs of the corpse so the law might use them to find out who Shaw really was. They took six pictures, showing the body in the coffin, and then being held upright. When the impromptu photo shoot was over, they lowered Shaw's remains back into the wooden box, dropped a partially filled whiskey bottle alongside, and said a short prayer. Volz

The day after John Shaw was killed in a gunfight,
cowboys dug up his grave to give him a final shot of whiskey.
SAM LOWE COLLECTION

Frank Ketchum

Frank Ketchum (left) and another man pose
with the body of John Shaw (center).
SAM LOWE COLLECTION

unloaded the camera and told one of the men to give the film to the sheriff. Subdued and even sobered by the macabre event, the cowboys and gamblers returned to Winslow, but the lawman never got the film. Instead, it was turned over to a local attorney who had prints made from each of the six negatives. The prints were handed down through his family until they wound up on display in a Winslow tavern, and then were turned over to historians.

But the weirdness wasn't over.

The surviving robber later told officials that his name wasn't really "Smythe," it was "Smith." And after he was sentenced to time in the territorial prison at Yuma, officials discovered that he had been there before—as William Evans. He had served six years of a ten-year sentence for robbery and was paroled in 1903. This time, he served another nine years before being pardoned in 1914.

Then there was another twist. It happened seven months after the gunfight at Canyon Diablo.

Deputy Sheriff Pemberton, whose well-aimed bullet had saved Sheriff Houck's life during the shootout, got drunk and killed Marshal Joe Giles during an argument in the Parlor Saloon in Winslow. Pemberton was losing heavily at the roulette wheel and became angry when Walter Darling, the croupier, refused to let him raise his bet. Drunk and enraged, Pemberton whipped out his six-shooter and fired. The bullet missed Darling and smashed into the wall. Just then, Marshal Giles walked into the saloon and tried to reason with Pemberton, who was already aiming a second shot at the frightened Darling.

Pemberton responded by whirling around and pumping five shots into the marshal's midsection. Although mortally wounded, Giles managed to draw and wildly empty his weapon. None of his shots hit anyone in the saloon. Pemberton ran from the bar and gave himself up to the town constable. Houck then took command. Because he was indebted to Pemberton, Houck arrested his deputy but refused to charge him. He also let Pemberton freely roam the streets. This enraged the citizens of Winslow. They brought pressure locally, then appealed to higher authorities to correct what they viewed a misplaced loyalty. Pemberton was arrested and stood trial in Prescott. After his lawyers argued that he was temporarily insane because of alcohol, a jury found him guilty of second-degree murder. He was sentenced to twenty-five years in prison, but served only a portion of it before being pardoned. By 1929, he was back living in Winslow and remained there until his death.

And Houck's loyalty carried a price. He lost the next election by a landslide.

There's little left of Canyon Diablo. The harsh winds common to the high desert continue to erode fragments of buildings and have long since covered the final resting places of those who died so violently. Only one marker remains in what was once a cemetery and, ironically, it designates the grave of the only man who died a natural death there.

In the classic words of the late Cecil Calvin Richardson, a former Coconino County sheriff who explored and wrote about the area:

A cold north wind sweeps out of the Painted Desert now and washes the rubble with an icy hand. Less than a mile to the south, eyes strained with staring into vast, empty highway distances, [watch as] another tide of westbound pilgrims in wagons of glass and steel, flash unconcernedly by on Interstate 40, leaving the ghosts on Boothill little with which to console themselves.

The original bridge, the span responsible for the creation of Canyon Diablo, is also gone. Only the concrete pilings that once supported it remain. It had a speed restriction of ten miles per hour, which caused traffic delays. The Santa Fe Railroad decided it was time to get rid of the bottlenecks and built a new bridge just north of the old one. Opened in 1947, it measures 544 feet across and includes a 300-foot hinged arch with 120-foot spans on either side. High speed trains now rush across it at up to seventy miles per hour.

The city of Winslow, where this historic episode began, has scrapped and survived despite suffering severe economic losses in the 1980s. During that era, the fabled Route 66, which once carried cars, trucks, and buses through the heart of town, was replaced by Interstate 40, a freeway that carries cars, trucks, and buses a few miles to the north at seventy-five miles per hour. Also, railroad passenger service was terminated.

But the citizens rallied. They built the world's only Standin' on the Corner in Winslow Arizona Park to memorialize a line from the song, "Take It Easy," that tells about a young man standing on the corner while a girl in a flatbed truck slows down to check him out. State officials initially scoffed at the idea, but the small area has become a major tourist attraction that draws hundreds of people who would normally drive right past Winslow if the park weren't there.

Also on the plus side is the La Posada, a former Harvey House that once served hungry rail passengers. It was one of several eating establishments/hotels built by the Fred Harvey Company in the late 1800s along the Atchison, Topeka & Santa Fe Railway route. After the passengers stopped coming, the hotel/restaurant was converted into office space by the railroad, but then was scheduled for demolition. Once again, the citizens rallied. They wrote grants, got some fix-up money and were able to convince Allen Affeldt, a California entrepreneur, to buy and restore the structure. He did, and now it draws tourists and diners from all across the nation.

The Wigwam Saloon didn't survive, however. It was torn down in the 1940s.

CHAPTER FOURTEEN

Giovanni Vigliotto:
His March to the Altar
Turned into a Stampede

In March 1983, the jokes circulating around the Maricopa County Courthouse in Phoenix during an unusual bigamy and fraud case included this one:

Question: What has 210 legs, 105 broken hearts, and no money?
Answer: Giovanni Vigliotto's wives.

Giovanni Vigliotto was on trial because he was a record-setting marryin' man. By his own calculations, he wooed, won, and wed 105 women. This created some major problems other than the obvious ones of wearing out his wedding suit and the cost of buying anniversary cards. One was that he never divorced any of his wives. Second, as soon as he took a new bride, he ran off and never returned. And third, when he ran off, he took her money and belongings with him.

Equally amazing was the fact that Vigliotto, by the usual criteria, was hardly a prize catch. He had an oversize nose, puffy lips, and a beer belly, and his wardrobe consisted primarily of well-worn blue jeans and tennis shoes. But he was a smooth talker and a good listener, and a surprising number of women found him irresistible.

His victims were single women—spinsters, divorcees, or widows. It didn't matter to him, as long as they had money. They were easy prey because they were lonely and he had a knack for comforting them because he was, some said later, honest, exciting, and compassionate.

But honesty and a sympathetic ear were merely tools, and Vigliotto was highly skilled in using them to pry earthly goods from the vulnerable and unsuspecting. In the end, all it brought him was jail time and an early death.

He did most of his damage over a twenty-year span that began in the early 1960s, but his life prior to that remains a mystery, outside of the fact that he was born on April 3, 1929. He told some of the women that he was born in Sicily and, while still a teenager, was captured by German soldiers who forced him to watch as they raped his mother and four sisters. To others, he was a veteran of both the Greek and British armies, a secret agent brought to the United States by the Central Intelligence Agency, a former Mafia don, a wealthy cowboy, or a millionaire who owned a big boat. He rarely used the same name more than once.

When Vigliotto was finally brought to trial, US Marshal William Harrison told reporters, "We've heard he's had more than one hundred twenty aliases. We've confirmed seventeen." Harrison added that Vigliotto boasted he had wives in eight foreign countries, and often gloated over their naivety. "He liked to write to them, telling them about what sort of pickin's they were," the marshal said. "It was all a game to him."

The truth may be that Vigliotto was actually Fred Jiff, born in Louisiana. He was a flea market trader who traveled around the country buying and selling a variety of items. He adopted several aliases as part of his plan to entice women because "Fred Jiff" didn't have as much sex appeal as an exotic Mediterranean or European name. After selecting a prospective new wife, Vigliotto told her that he was just working in the area but had a permanent residence in some faraway state. After they became acquainted, he'd ask her to invest in one of his enterprises, and if they agreed, he would follow with a wedding proposal. Sometimes, it took only days to implement his strategy; others held out for months. But in the end, most fell for his charm, sincerity, and apparent willingness to provide them with a better life.

After the nuptials, Vigliotto convinced the women to sell their own homes so they could buy one together and live happily ever after. Then he packed all their belongings into a moving van or a truck and drove away, promising to contact them as soon as he reached the destination they had selected. He never called. Soon

Giovanni Vigliotto's demise was major news both in Arizona and nationwide.
MONTAGE BY AUTHOR

after that, he was selling their household goods and jewelry at flea markets a long distance away. Some called the authorities; many were too embarrassed to file a complaint and marked it off as one of life's cruel lessons.

Joan Bacarella of Englishtown, New Jersey, was one of his victims. Vigliotto proposed a day after they met. She was separated from her husband; he urged her to get a divorce so they could marry. She accepted his proposition and it cost her. Her new husband quickly borrowed $1,600 in cash and loaded up $40,000 worth of inventory from the clothing shop she owned, promising quick returns on both. He never arrived at the motel where Bacarella waited with her mother and three children.

Sharon Clark of Angola, Indiana, also fell for his charm. But not right away.

"He was dressed like a rich cowboy, with two big gold bracelets and a chain with gold toothpicks," she said during an interview conducted by Cable Neuhaus, a writer for *People* magazine. She said she didn't like him because he was rude and demeaning, and he insisted that she give him her full attention. But he was persistent. He told Clark he was "a lonely, unhappy man" but that she brought him great pleasure. On her birthday, he gave her yellow roses taped to a case of beer.

Then he started crying while telling her about his abused childhood. "He cried and I began to see the softness in him," Clark said later. He proposed. She turned him down. Two months later, he talked her into buying a van together, and then proposed again. She accepted—not only his proposal, but also an offer to move to Texas where they would form a partnership and open a chain of antiques stores.

"I married him because I knew I'd never be bored," she told the reporter. "He spoke seven languages. He said he'd been all over the world. Every time he talked, he excited me."

Over the next few months, he talked a lot. He talked her into marrying him in a hippie-style wedding (she was barefoot) in a wooded area in Tennessee. He talked her into believing he had a dark past, which is why he kept a gun under his pillow. He talked her into weird sexual practices, which she didn't like but accepted because "he said I was a witch and had cast a spell on him."

He continued talking. He talked Clark's mother into moving to Texas with them and talked her out of her jewelry. He talked a young flea marketer named John Boslett into going to work for him. He also talked Boslett into investing in his venture and said he would run the business while he and his new bride were on vacation. He talked Sharon into selling a house she owned, and talked her into giving him the proceeds by promising her she'd have big houses once they got to Texas, and that they'd travel anywhere she wanted to go.

He also talked her into giving him $11,000 in cash and let him pile an estimated $44,000 in goods into the van he had purchased with her money. But, he said prior to his departure, they wouldn't go to Texas right away. He said he had business in Ohio, and told her to meet him in Detroit. When she arrived at the designated place in the Motor City, she found instructions to drive to Toronto where he'd be waiting. But he didn't show up in either city. He had disappeared, four months after they were married. Almost everything she owned went with him. She was left with eight dollars in cash, a beat-up old car, and a tankful of gasoline.

She realized then what so many had realized before her: She had been had.

While Clark was mourning her losses, Vigliotto hooked up with Patricia Ann Gardiner, a real estate agent from Mesa, Arizona. They met at a local swap meet; they were married eight days later. During the brief courtship, Vigliotto bragged that he had $49 million in savings. He also told his new conquest that he owned the *Queen Mary,* the former ocean liner that had been converted into a hotel and was now docked at Long Beach, California. It wasn't long before he persuaded Gardiner to sell her home in Mesa and move to California with him. They set off in two vehicles. Vigliotto drove the van, which carried about $36,000 worth of the cash and valuables she had entrusted to his care; she and her pet poodle followed in her car. They became separated during the long drive to San Diego so she went on alone and arrived at the hotel as planned. Then she waited. And waited. Eventually, she realized she'd been taken.

But unlike so many before, Patricia Ann Gardiner wasn't about to let him get away with it.

Neither was Sharon Clark.

Gardiner pressed criminal charges and began tracking him down by scouring the countryside for flea markets where she thought he might appear. Clark also set out in hot pursuit of the

Lothario they had inadvertently shared, and Giovanni Vigliotto's days as a con man, fraud artist, and bigamist were numbered.

Clark contacted Boslett, who was still smarting over his losses, so he readily agreed to help. He hitchhiked from Florida, and the chase began. Among the few possessions she retained from their relationship was a road map Vigliotto used to locate outlets for his ill-gotten merchandise. He had circled several flea market towns from Missouri to Louisiana to Florida. The two hunters scraped together some traveling money, bought a used van, and began the hunt. They figured their quarry would head south because it was warmer there. A multitude of flea markets would be in operation to service the needs of the bargain-seeking winter visitors who make annual treks to warmer climes. Clark said they lived like bums, frequently eating bean sandwiches and washing them down with beer while they checked flea markets in Missouri, Louisiana, Mississippi, Alabama, and Florida.

They pursued their quarry for about three months until one day in December 1981, when they spotted him working an outdoor market in Panama City, Florida. He was selling Patricia Gardiner's furniture. Clark's first impulse was to accost Vigliotto and "knock the hell out of him," but Boslett warned her that he might be armed. So she called authorities while Boslett slashed the tires on Vigliotto's van, which they recognized because it was the same one he drove while leaving them stranded in Indiana. Less than an hour later the cross-country Romeo was under arrest. Days later, he was extradited to Arizona to face charges filed by Gardiner.

Clark and Boslett had won, but at great cost. They were down to their last three dollars, living on popcorn, and were convinced they'd never get any of their money back. They were right about the assumption. None of the money Vigliotto stole from his wives was ever returned to any of them. Marshal Harrison told the media, "We don't know where all the money is. Vigliotto supposedly has a motor home somewhere that's a rolling Fort Knox, but no one has been able to find it." No one ever did.

His trial began on March 28, 1983, under a near-circus atmosphere. Courtroom spectators brought snacks and drinks and laughed aloud at some of the testimony. Vigliotto became a media celebrity and earned a spot in the *Guinness Book of Records* as "the world's most married but never divorced" man. The jokes about extra wives were repeated so often that they became stale.

Gardiner, the apparent 105th wife, testified for the prosecution. She told the jury about meeting Vigliotto and falling under his spell. "He looked right into my face and eyes," she said. "I liked that honest trait." But she also recalled how she lost the $36,000 and how she and her poodle were the only ones to arrive in San Diego at the appointed time and place.

Clark and Bacarella also testified against their former husband.

Bacarella told the jury she realized that "my prince had turned into a frog" after she was left broke and stranded while Vigliotto made off with about $45,000 of her money and merchandise. Clark described her three-month search after ending up broke and abandoned in Detroit.

Vigliotto denied defrauding any of his wives. He argued that things had been blown way out of proportion, and that he was misunderstood. During one rambling statement, he claimed that "it was always the women who popped the question." He presented himself as a sort of Walter Mitty, the miserable daydreamer in the James Thurber novel who imagines himself in a variety of heroic roles to escape his less-than-perfect real life. And he wondered aloud if he was the only person who ever gave in to such fantasies.

During interviews before and after the trial, he declared that he loved women because they gave him a chance to "escape into a beautiful dream (into) a world of fantasy" where he wasn't short, dumpy and homely. He felt hurt, he said, that some of his wives were now saying bad things about him, and asked, "If they really feel that way, why did they marry me?" He maintained that his manner toward them was simply his normal behavior.

While talking with columnist Tom Fitzpatrick of the *New Times,* a Phoenix weekly, Vigliotto complained, "They say I mesmerize people. That's just not true. They charge me with adopting a courtly manner to manipulate these women . . . I never realized there was any other way to treat a woman than the way I do. Is it wrong for a man to hold open the door for a woman to pass through? Is it wrong to buy them flowers? If the rest of the men in the United States don't treat women that way, then I'm sorry for the women in this country. No wonder so many of them were anxious to marry me."

In his story, Fitzpatrick said Vigliotto then made fists of both his hands and pounded them against his chest and said, in a rising voice, "I love women! And I think I love them because they bring me out of myself."

Besides that, he added, "They give me a chance to escape into a beautiful dream . . . into a world of fantasy. They take me on a wonderful trip to a wonderful place where everyone is in love . . . Does that make me the world's worst human being? . . . Must I be persecuted for having fantasies? Am I the only one who has ever had dreams and sought to live them out? . . ."

Toward the end of the interview, Vigliotto declared, "I have lived more in my years than the average man would if he lived a hundred lifetimes."

After the trial started, presiding judge Rufus Coulter asked Vigliotto if he could remember the names of the women he had married. He asked for a pen and spent the lunch recess writing, then submitted a list of 105 names. They were, he said, the women he had married and left in eighteen states and nine foreign countries. The last name was Patricia Ann Gardiner.

He also admitted many aliases but couldn't remember most of them. They were chosen, he said, to fit the role he was playing at the time. As the trial continued, it became more of a theatrical event than a legal proceeding. Vigliotto's antics irritated Judge Coulter and prosecuting attorney Dave Stoller. And he also alienated Richard Steiner, his own defense lawyer, when he told him the 105 names were just a joke.

Impressed by his endurance and guile, but not swayed by any of it, the jury of eight women and four men took only twenty-four minutes to find Vigliotto guilty on twenty-eight counts of fraud and six counts of bigamy. He was sentenced to twenty-eight years in prison and fined $336,000. He glared at Judge Coulter and accused him of practicing "hang 'em high justice," then was escorted back to his jail cell to wait for his trip to the state penitentiary at Florence.

After the trial, Gardiner told reporters that she felt sorry for the other women who had been betrayed. "I don't think they fell for him," she said. "They found someone who told them what they needed and wanted to hear at that time in their lives."

But Clark expressed little sympathy for those who had loved and lost. "I figure 90 percent of them deserved it," she told the magazine writer. "I deserved it, too, because I was so gullible, but I'm different from most women. Some of them should have gone and done something."

On April 8, 1983, Giovanni Vigliotto, sometimes known as Nikolai Peruskov, became Inmate Number 047038, a male Caucasian who stood 62 inches tall, weighed 220 pounds, and had black hair and hazel eyes.

A little more than five months later, prison officials searched his maximum security cell and removed ten boxes of "miscellaneous legal materials." Vigliotto claimed they were transcripts from his trial and newspaper clippings pertaining to his case, and said they were necessary for the appeal he planned to file. He sued Major Frank Terry, the officer who directed the search, and two prison guards, arguing that the search deprived him of his right to access of the courts, and violated the Eighth Amendment's prohibition of cruel and unusual punishment. The defendants argued that the materials were contraband. They were boxed and put into storage, and Vigliotto was given three days to find a place to keep them or they would be destroyed. The girlfriend of another inmate picked up the boxes and sent them back to a Vigliotto acquaintance in Michigan. They were later shipped back to Arizona, but Steiner, Vigliotto's public defender, refused to pay the freight costs so the boxes went back into storage and were then lost.

The modern-day Casanova represented himself at the hearing because, he said, the court-appointed attorney didn't have his best interests at heart. He wasn't much better at practicing law than he was at finding true love because the district court ruled against him, declaring that "the search did not violate defendant's Eighth Amendment rights." He then appealed his sentence and again acted as his own attorney. He lost that one, also.

Vigliotto spent eight years in the Arizona prison. During that time, he began writing a book about his life that he hoped would become a television special. A chemical company allegedly offered him one million dollars if he'd endorse a potency drug. Several women proposed marriage; several others formed a group intent on proving his innocence so he could get a new trial. But nothing came of any of them.

Vigliotto, a diabetic, suffered a debilitating stroke in 1988, and died in the Maricopa County Medical Center on February 3, 1991, following a brain hemorrhage. Patricia O'Connor, a Phoenix private investigator who led a legal effort to free him, was in the room when the life support ventilator was disconnected. "He put up a valiant fight," she said. "He never, never gave up hope." She also claimed that poor medical care in prison exacerbated his medical problems. After the stroke, he was confined to a wheelchair and spent the next two years being shuttled between the county hospital and prison.

His death drew front-page stories in the local press as well as notices in such major publications as the *Los Angeles Times, Boston Globe, Time* magazine, and the *New York Times*. All of them pointed out that he had married 105 women and never divorced any of them.

The supermarket tabloid *Weekly World News* was much less subtle when it announced his demise with a front page headline that screamed: "Too Much Sex Kills Man with 105 Wives!" The story below quoted an unnamed prison doctor as saying, "If ever a man was killed by too much sex, it was Giovanni. The death certificate may not say so, but this man was destroyed physically and mentally by too many romps in the sack."

That report could justifiably be viewed with suspicion, however, because the same tabloid also published stories about P'lod, an extraterrestrial who had an affair with Hillary Clinton; a giant mutant hog that terrorized Arkansas; and Bat Boy, a half-bat, half-human superhero.

Although he never finished the book that was to become the basis for a television special, Vigliotto did have a posthumous moment on the tube in 1995 when the series *Tough Target* featured him in an episode entitled "Romeo." He was portrayed by Dick Gjonola, who also appeared as the original Burger King in commercials from 1980 through 1983.

CHAPTER FIFTEEN

Andy Cooper Blevins:
Rustler, Murderer, and Shootout Victim

The second page of the *Holbrook Arizona Guide* features a map denoting the city's major historic sites, along with instructions on how to reach them. The guide informs visitors that there are 108 stops along the 2.5-mile tour, and that the buildings marked in solid black are the original structures. The Navajo County Courthouse carries the honor of being the first site listed.

Some of the others include the Masonic Lodge (No. 4), the McAllister House (No. 11), the J&J Trading Post (No. 19), and perhaps the most famous (or infamous, depending upon the particular point of view), the Blevins House (No. 26). It was the scene of a bloody shootout that locals claim was as historically important as the gunfight down at the OK Corral in Tombstone.

The guide book opens with a brief history of Holbrook. The first sentence reads:

"Flood, fire, bullets and blood marked Holbrook's early days, yet from these struggles Holbrook's citizens would go on to make their mark in Arizona's history . . ."

And bullets and blood were the prime factors in the shootout that made the former residence of the Blevins family a matter of historic importance.

The building is located on Joy Nevin Avenue, about a block and a half east of Navajo Boulevard, the city's main drag, and just down the street from the White Saloon, where members of the notorious Hashknife Outfit once slaked their thirst and behaved in rowdy fashion. The house, a small wooden-frame structure, was built sometime after 1860. The basic shape remains the same, but additions have been made to the back, long after the

The house where Andy Cooper Blevins and two others died is now a senior citizens center and thrift store in Holbrook.
SAM LOWE PHOTO

episode that made it subject matter for historians. It was purchased by the city in 1970 and now serves as an extended-care facility and thrift store.

A couple of trees shelter the house from the dry, hot winds that sweep across Holbrook in the summer. A flagpole rises in the front yard, near a bronze plaque embedded in a piece of sandstone. The writing on the plaque tells about the historic Wagon Road that once passed by, but makes no mention of what happened at the house itself. Nor are there are any visible signs that a large amount of blood was shed at the site one day in a long-ago September.

Andy Cooper Blevins died there on September 4, 1887. So did his brother, Sam Houston Blevins, and Mose Roberts, a family friend. All three were shot by Sheriff Commodore Perry Owens in a gunfight that lasted less than five minutes.

It was inevitable that Owens and Andy Cooper Blevins would confront each other. Each one had achieved considerable notoriety in their respective undertakings—Blevins as a heartless criminal, Owens as a fearless lawman. They both arrived in Arizona in the 1880s and once rode together as cowhands. But later, after an alleged fallout over a woman, they chose widely divergent paths.

Blevins was born in 1861, the oldest son of Martin and Mary Blevins. He grew up in Texas, and became known as a bully who lorded over ranchers and sheepherders. By the time he reached age twenty-three, he was already a familiar face to Texas authorities. He allegedly killed a man, sold illegal whiskey to Indians, then was sent to prison for stealing horses. He escaped, became a wanted man, and began using the name of Andy Cooper in an attempt to confuse his pursuers.

His criminal behavior was a major reason for the family's move to Arizona Territory. With Texas lawmen continually on his trail because of charges ranging from assault to murder, he urged his father to pull up stakes and head west. The elder Blevins agreed. But if he thought relocating was going to change things, he was wrong. Shortly after their arrival, Andy and his four brothers—Charlie, Hampton, John, and Sam—allied themselves with the Graham factor in the Pleasant Valley War in eastern Arizona. More trouble would follow.

The conflict, also known as the Tonto Range War and the Tonto Basin War, began in 1882. It raged on for nearly a decade and took the lives of between nineteen and forty-five men. The principals were the Grahams and the Tewksburys, rival cattlemen who had a longstanding feud over water and grazing rights. There were conflicting reports about the reasons for the animosity. The two families had never gotten along well, and both sides accused the other of rustling cattle and stealing horses. Their dislike for each other

There are no known photographs of Andy Cooper Blevins.
This sketch by Arizona artist Marilee Lasch is based on an earlier
drawing done while Blevins was incarcerated in Texas.
MARILEE LASCH SKETCH

came to a head when the Tewksbury clan either decided to raise sheep along with cattle and brought in large flocks of the woolly creatures, or because they sided with other sheepherders simply because they didn't like the Grahams. Their rivals contended that the sheep grazed the land clean, leaving no forage for the cattle.

The first shot of the Tonto Range War was fired in February 1887 when a Navajo sheepherder employed by the Tewksburys was murdered. The herder was instructed by the Tewksburys to watch some sheep they had leased from the Daggs Brothers ranch in northeastern Arizona. Allegedly, the watchman drove his flock into the Mogollon Rim area, which had long been accepted as the vicinity where no sheep were allowed to graze. Tom Graham was blamed. According to historians, he not only killed the Navajo man with three bullets to the back, but also drove out or destroyed the sheep.

The situation went steadily downhill from there. William Graham was gunned down at his home the following August. Before he died, he identified Edwin Tewksbury as his assailant. Over the next few years, a multitude of lynchings and unsolved murders claimed the lives of men from both factions. The crimes were often committed by men wearing masks. The feud lasted for more than a decade but the deadliest period was between 1886 and 1887, when members of both sides were gunned down or hanged, but no suspects were ever charged. The last known fatality occurred in 1892. The end result was that the two families involved were annihilated.

As the feud turned into a war, other settlers were drawn into the fray, many of them on the side of the Grahams because they also were upset with the influx of sheep onto their primary grazing lands. One of them was Fred Burnham, who was forced into the hostilities only because he sided with a friend.

Burnham, a nineteen-year-old cowboy, worked for Fred Wells, an area cattleman who treated his young hired hand almost as a son. Wells was in debt to financiers in Globe because he borrowed heavily to start his own herd. Although he had no stake in the ongoing conflict, his creditors did. They demanded that he either help drive off the Tewksbury cattle or forfeit his own. He refused; the creditors sent lawmen to confiscate his cattle. Wells and his family rounded up their cows and began moving them to higher ground in the mountains where they'd be safe, not only from the law, but also from those who were shooting at each other down below in Pleasant Valley.

The two deputies caught up with the entourage and, during the confrontation that followed, one of them was shot and killed. The family held the other lawman hostage until they reached their destination, then released him. The deputy hurried back to

Globe to spread the word. Posses organized to hunt down the killers, with particular emphasis on Fred Burnham because he was an outsider, whereas the Wells family members had a long history in the area.

Burnham left the mountains and headed toward Globe, where he had friends who might provide him with shelter. On the way, he encountered George Dixon, a bounty hunter, who found the young cowboy hiding in a cave. Dixon put a gun to Burnham's head and ordered him outside. But as they left the cave, Dixon was shot and killed by Coyotero, a White Mountain Apache who had been tracking the gunslinger because of crimes he had committed against the tribe. Burnham grabbed his rifle and killed his savior, then made his way back to Globe, where he hid in the home of a friend. Using a variety of aliases, he escaped from the war and the Tonto Basin and settled in California.

Later on, Burnham became a world traveler and adventurer. He served with the British Army in colonial Africa, became involved in espionage, conservation, and writing, and befriended Robert Baden-Powell, the founder of the international Scouting movement. In his later years, Burnham recounted his involvement in the Pleasant Valley War in his memoirs, titled *Scouting on Two Continents*.

The Wells family escaped any further trouble. Others weren't so lucky.

After the death of the sheepherder, and despite all the evidence pointing to Tom Graham as the killer, the *Prescott Miner* placed all the blame for that incident, and many others, directly on Andy Cooper Blevins. On January 6, 1886, the newspaper reported that Cooper had killed two more Navajos as they were trying to steal a horse, and concluded the story with the observation that the US Army should hire him to hunt Apaches. By April 1887, Cooper was wanted in Texas, New Mexico, and at least one county in Arizona, and almost every report about horse theft mentioned him as a probable suspect.

The news stories also noted that Cooper often rode with the Hashknife Outfit, a gang of cowpokes and gunslingers employed by the Aztec Land and Cattle Company to oversee the forty thousand head of cattle they brought into the area in 1884. They took their name from the company's brand, which resembled the knife used by rangeland cooks while preparing chuckwagon grub. Many of them were fugitives from Texas and New Mexico, and when they weren't tending cattle and protecting Aztec's interests, they were in Holbrook shooting up the town and its residents. An estimated twenty-five people were shot and killed during the Hashknife gang's reign of terror.

On August 1, 1887, Martin Blevins disappeared while searching for stray horses. According to a widely accepted story, his son Hampton and a friend went to look for him. They never found the missing man, but lawmen later discovered shallow graves containing the bodies of the younger Blevins and the other man. Everyone assumed all three were victims of the range war.

But in a family history written by Ruth Blevins Chesley, one of John Blevins's granddaughters, Hampton and two Hashknife members, identified only as Tucker and Payne, stopped at a Tewksbury ranch and asked for lunch, despite the enmities. She wrote, "Little did they know that their every move was being watched and that death was riding with them."

When the rancher, Jim Tewksbury, refused to feed them, they turned their horses to ride away. "As soon as their backs were turned," she wrote, "Tucker said jets of flame and smoke spurted from the half open doorway (and) Hampton Blevins swayed limply in the saddle as a bullet crashed through his brain. In the next instant, Payne's horse crashed down in agony of death, pinning the rider's legs to the ground. As he struggled to get free from his dying horse, a bullet from Jim Tewksbury's rifle clipped off his ear. As he freed himself and started to run for shelter, that deadly rifle cut him down and he too lay in the dust with Hampton."

She said her information came from relatives, friends, and her grandmother, Eva Blevins. However, since her account made no mention of how Tucker escaped the gunfire, it was generally considered hearsay.

Regardless of which version is the most reliable, Andy Cooper Blevins flew into a rage and vowed revenge.

On September 1, 1887, Cooper, his brother Charlie, and gunmen from the Graham faction surrounded a cabin owned by the Tewksburys and wantonly murdered John Tewksbury Jr. and William Jacobs as they worked with their horses in the farmyard. They continued firing at the building for hours while those inside watched in horror as the bodies of the dead men decomposed under the hot desert sun. The attackers stopped shooting only long enough to allow Mrs. Tewksbury time to dig shallow graves and bury the two victims. Once she returned to the cabin, the gunfire resumed.

Two days later, while drinking in a Holbrook saloon, Cooper openly bragged that he had killed both men. He also boasted that there wasn't a sheriff in the West who was foolish enough to arrest him because they were all afraid of him. It wasn't long before word reached Sheriff Owens. He already had a warrant for Cooper on a charge of stealing horses, but had never served it. When the Apache County Board of Supervisors ordered him to arrest Cooper or be removed from office, Owens said he was reluctant to do so because he thought it might end in the deaths of one or both of them. But, tired of the insinuations that he was a coward, Owens figured this would be a good time to take action.

So he went to the Blevins house on September 4, 1887.

Commodore Perry Owens had already established himself as a no-nonsense lawman. He was born in Tennessee in 1853, and acquired his unusual name because his birth date was the fortieth anniversary of his namesake's triumph over the British naval forces on Lake Erie during the War of 1812, and his mother was a history buff with a longstanding admiration for the war hero. Despite his name, or perhaps inspired by it, Owens became an expert shot with both rifle and pistol, worked as a cowboy on Texas ranches, hired on as a buffalo hunter to supply meat for railroad crews, and arrived in Arizona in 1881. In 1887, he was elected sheriff of Apache County but he didn't receive the respect usually associated with such a job title. He let his hair grow to his shoulders, dressed in a fringed buckskin jacket and silver-studded leather chaps, and wore a wide-brimmed felt-top hat, all uncommon traits on the frontier. When word got out that he also bathed at least once a week, many of the townspeople considered him a bit too prissy for the job.

But nobody said as much, at least not to his face. Owens had already killed two cattle rustling suspects and his reputation as a sharpshooter was widespread. He wore twin six-shooters, one on each hip, and was deadly with both, regardless of which hand he used. His effectiveness with a rifle was on the same level.

It was a relatively calm Sunday when Sheriff Owens, with the warrant in his pocket, rode into town from the county seat at St. Johns, looking for Andy Cooper. The outlaw knew he was coming; his brother John had spotted the lawman and warned Andy, who was inside the Blevins house along with several other people who had gathered for Sunday dinner. Among them were Mary Blevins (Andy's mother and Martin Blevins's widow); her daughter Artemisia; John Blevins, his wife Eva, and their infant son; Sam Blevins; family friends Mose Roberts and Amanda Gladden, and her baby.

Owens walked to the front door and knocked. Cooper opened it, but then tried to slam it shut when he saw the sheriff. But Owens had a foot inside the door and told the suspect he had a warrant for his arrest on a horse-stealing charge. He ordered Cooper to step outside; when he refused and apparently reached for his six-gun, Owens fired a single shot from his rifle. It hit Cooper in the stomach. Another door opened and John Blevins took a shot at Owens from about four feet away. He missed but the bullet struck and killed Cooper's horse, which had been tied to a nearby tree.

Owens fired a second shot. It caught John Blevins in the shoulder and sent him to the floor. Then Cooper hauled himself to a window and aimed his gun at Owens, but never got to fire it. The lawman's third shot ripped through the wall of the house and into Cooper's hip. Screaming wildly, Sam Blevins, the youngest of the brothers at fifteen, grabbed Cooper's gun and raced out the front door, cursing and swearing vengeance against Owens. His mother reached out in a desperate attempt to stop him; it was too late. The fourth round from the sheriff's rifle was also deadly. The boy died in his mother's arms. The lawman then retreated to a nearby stable. Seconds later, Mose Roberts climbed out a bedroom window, holding a pistol. Owens fired again; the bullet hit Roberts in the shoulder and tore through his body. He staggered back into the house and fell to the floor, mortally wounded.

The entire episode had taken about three minutes.

Owens calmly returned to the livery stable. He told bystanders that he "got all of them," retrieved his horse and rode away. Once the firing stopped, friends and neighbors rushed to the Blevins' house; they were horrified by the bloodshed they saw inside. Andy Cooper and Mose Roberts lay dying on the floor. John Blevins was clutching his wounded shoulder. Mary Blevins was still holding the body of her youngest son. Amanda Gladden, Eva Blevins, and their babies were all splattered with blood. Cooper lived for about another eight hours; Roberts died eleven days later after testifying at a coroner's inquest that Owens had never called for him to surrender.

John Blevins recovered from his wound, but was found guilty of assault with intent to murder Owens in 1888. He was sentenced to five years in prison, but then was pardoned by the governor before serving any time. The pardon reached Owens by telegram at Flagstaff as he was escorting his prisoner to the Yuma Territorial Prison by train. Owens released the man immediately, leaving him stranded in Flagstaff without money or means to get home. He arrived in Holbrook several days later, emaciated and half-frozen. Charlie Blevins, the other brother, wasn't there during the deadly shootout, but was killed later that same month in a gun battle with lawmen in Young.

A coroner's jury cleared Owens, despite testimony from the dying Roberts, and from Mary Blevins, who had lost two sons in an attack she claimed was unprovoked.

Later that month, Sheriff George Mulverson of Prescott led a posse in pursuit of Charlie Blevins and John and Tom Graham, and found them in Young. The sheriff demanded that they surrender but, typical of the times, they refused and drew their guns. When the shooting was over, John Graham and Charlie Blevins lay dead.

Tom Graham escaped, but he became the last recorded fatality of the hostilities when he was shot and killed in Tempe in August 1892. Before he died, he identified Edwin Tewksbury as the shooter and several witnesses backed up his claim. Tewksbury was arrested and went to trial twice. The first one ended in a hung jury. He was convicted after the second but the verdict was deferred due to a legal technicality. The case was dismissed in 1895.

Edwin Tewksbury, the last man directly involved in the Pleasant Valley War, died in Globe in April 1904 of natural causes. John Blevins, who had survived the war and the shootout in his home, died from injuries suffered in a car accident near Tucson on May 23, 1929.

Although he had rid the territory of one of its more unsavory characters, Owens did not emerge from the incident as a hero. Rather, the residents of Apache County began to fear him and pointed out that he had shot into a house occupied by women and children. And, they said, he had killed a boy. As a result, Owens did not seek reelection in 1888. He became a railroad guard, and then was appointed the first sheriff of Navajo County shortly after it was created by dividing Apache County in half. He died in May 1919, still haunted by the ghosts of the men—and the boy—he had killed.

Holbrook is no longer a wild and rowdy frontier town. The dry summer winds still reshape the landscape but the crime rate is almost nonexistent. The Hashknife Outfit is still around, but today they're a law-abiding ceremonial group whose members carry the mail by horseback from Holbrook to Scottsdale once a year. Andy Cooper Blevins, his brother Sam, and Mose Roberts are all buried in the Holbrook Cemetery. Their bodies were

Andy Cooper Blevins and his brother are
buried beneath a sandstone marker.
SAM LOWE PHOTO

moved from their original graves in the 1930s due to a highway realignment.

Their current graves lie about a mile from the house where they met their fate. In 1980, descendants of John Blevins held a family reunion and had the three victims' names chiseled into a large sandstone square. They placed it on the graves as a headstone.

CHAPTER SIXTEEN
Augustine Chacon:
Robin Hood or Murderer?

The history of the Old West is filled with many a tale about bad men who weren't really all *that* bad, or men who turned outlaw because of injustices heaped upon their innocent souls. Augustine Chacon wasn't one of them. He was just plain bad.

He bragged that there were thirty notches on his gun, but also claimed he'd murdered as many as fifty men on both sides of the Arizona-Mexico border. He escaped hanging twice, broke out of jail frequently, and had no remorse about killing a former friend.

Despite that, Chacon had a loyal following of both men and women, who elevated him to the status of a frontier Robin Hood and aided his flights from incarceration. When he was sentenced to hang, they fought the death penalty. And after he died, they rejected the coroner's report and insisted that their hero had been revived and was still among them.

But he wasn't.

Chacon's story is strangely familiar because he, like many of his peers, worked both sides of the law. Born in 1861 in the Mexican state of Sonora, he became a peace officer in Tigre, a small Sonoran town. During that period, he also became proficient at rustling cattle and horses, then selling them on the other side of the border. It became a pattern throughout most of his life. The Mexican authorities couldn't chase him into Arizona Territory, and territorial lawmen had no jurisdiction in Sonora, so he crossed from one side to the other with ease and little fear of being caught.

Chacon was the epitome of tall, dark and handsome. He was nicknamed "El Peludo" (Spanish for "the hairy one") and wore a fierce mustache from his late teens until the day he died. Women were seduced by his swarthy good looks; men rode with him out of admiration and respect. He recruited thugs, robbers, and outlaws

Augustine Chacon's life as a murderer came to an end in Solomonville.
SCOTTSDALE CC SOUTHWEST STUDIES

in Sonora, rode across the border to commit crimes in Arizona, then hightailed it back to his native land where they'd go into seclusion until their next lawless foray.

By the time he was in his late twenties, Chacon was well known and feared across the territory. He pistol-whipped drivers and passengers while robbing a stagecoach near Phoenix, and killed four people during a holdup in Jerome. But in 1888, he also used his skills as a cowboy and went to work for Ben Ollney, a rancher near Morenci. It turned out to be another murderous excursion when he got into a salary dispute with his boss, drew his gun, and mortally wounded him. As the rancher lay dying, other cowpokes raced to the scene. Chacon shot and killed five of them. Area lawmen quickly organized a posse and chased the killer into the hills. They wounded him in the arm, but Chacon gunned four of them down before escaping into the Chihuahuan Desert and back into Mexico.

Just a few months later, he was spotted near Fort Apache in south central Arizona. A vigilante gang subdued him, threw him in jail, and vowed to end his crime spree with an early morning trip to the hanging tree. But when dawn came, Chacon was gone. In his place, the would-be execution squad found the hacksaw blades someone had smuggled into his cell. Rumors spread that the rancher's daughter was his accomplice, but the accusations never got beyond the gossip stage.

By this time, Chacon was wanted for murder, robbery, assault, and rustling. Aware that his days as a free man would be severely shortened if he reappeared in Arizona Territory, he spent the next several years in Mexico, making only a few nighttime raids into the area around the border town of Naco. But apparently, things must have gotten pretty dull in Mexico because by 1894, he was back in Morenci.

He found work on ranches and in the mines, and quickly established himself as an unelected leader of the poor Mexican laborers. He helped them stage midnight raids on neighboring ranches to steal cattle, and then helped them butcher the cows to supplant their meager diets. What they didn't take for themselves, they sold to local meat markets.

But the financial rewards from working and rustling were low and the hours were a hindrance to his lifestyle. There had to be an easier way to make money, Chacon figured, so he went back to life as a full-time criminal. Although no one could ever prove it, and no charges were ever brought, he was suspected of murdering two young miners and stealing their guns, money, and equipment. Then he moved south to Tucson where he had a run-in with Texas John Slaughter, the sheriff of Cochise County and one of the toughest lawmen in Western history. Slaughter and Deputy Burt Alvord cornered Chacon in a tent outside of town and ordered him to surrender. He refused and ran out through the back flap of the tent. Slaughter got off one shot but missed. Chacon fled into the night.

Even though the territory was branded as a haven for outlaws, Chacon's list of safe places was dangerously low. He once again selected Morenci as one of them. It was not his smartest move.

Near midnight on December 18, 1895, Chacon and two associates—Pilar Luna and Dionicio Morales—waited in the darkness until Paul Becker, an employee at McCormack's general store, locked the doors and headed for a meal at a nearby saloon. Then they broke in and began looting the store. But the robbery was interrupted when Becker unexpectedly came back. They subdued him and ordered him to open the safe, but Becker refused, even when one of the robbers drove a six-inch blade into his side. He was able to escape and made his way back to the saloon where Deputy Alex Davis pulled the knife from his rib cage and learned what had happened. The robbers raced from the store and hid out in the home of Santiago Contrera. They were still there the next morning, when Davis and several deputized locals arrived and the shooting began.

The three criminals were flushed from the house and ran up a hill in back while the sounds and echoes of the gunfire roared through the community. One participant later said that more than three hundred shots had been fired. Two of them mortally wounded Luna and Morales as they attempted to get to their horses.

Morenci businessman Pablo Salcido was also shot and killed. He and Chacon had once been friends and Salcido convinced the lawmen that he could talk the outlaw into surrendering. Given permission, he walked toward the rocks where Chacon was hiding to make his appeal. Chacon stepped out from behind a boulder and invited his friend to approach. But as Salcido walked nearer, he took a bullet from Chacon's gun directly to the forehead.

When the firing resumed in all its fury, Chacon was wounded in the arm and chest and gave up. He was taken back to the Solomonville jail, considered by many to be the most insecure pokey in Arizona Territory. Chacon gave credence to the claim when he strolled out of his cell one night almost unnoticed. The jailers soon became aware of his absence and organized a search party. Chacon hid in a ditch but was captured when one of the searchers tripped over him. The following May, he was tried for the murder of Salcido, his onetime friend. Defense attorneys argued that Pilar Luna had fired the fatal shot before he himself was killed. The jury didn't buy it. Chacon was convicted and sentenced to death by hanging.

The execution was set for July 24, 1896, in Solomonville.

It didn't happen.

After being transferred to a jail in Tucson for security reasons, Chacon appealed to the territorial Supreme Court; the verdict was upheld. A group of citizens organized to protest the death penalty. Their anti–capital punishment stance was based on statistics that indicated wealthy Anglos were rarely put to death for crimes of any kind, but minorities were often marched to the gallows. In Solomonville, then the seat of Graham County, nine men had been hanged before Chacon's date with death. Three of them were Chinese, two were Mexican, two others were black, and one was an Apache. Only one was Anglo. The protesters petitioned to have the sentence reduced to life imprisonment. The request was denied. An area newspaper reported that there was "a sentiment in Graham County amounting almost to a religious fervor against hanging [Chacon]."

And, while being returned to Solomonville, Chacon attempted to escape by sawing through his handcuffs. The attempt failed. That, coupled with the protests and appeals, forced a delay in carrying out the sentence. The new date was set as June 18, 1897.

June 18, 1897, arrived.

Chacon wasn't there to take part in the main event.

Nine days earlier, he had managed to cut the shackles from both his wrists and ankles, then smashed holes into the adobe walls of his cell and sawed through the thick support beams to make a successful escape. Theories abounded. Some said friends had smuggled the necessary tools into the jail one by one, and he used them while his sympathetic Mexican cellmates sang loud songs and played raucous music to cover the noise. According to another version, a beautiful señorita had smuggled hacksaw blades into jail by hiding them in a Bible. That same woman, so the story goes, also lured the jailer into a back room where she seduced him while Chacon was getting away. Regardless of who was responsible, Chacon was free once more, and he stayed that way for about five years.

But his name popped up every time there was a crime in the area, particularly if it involved murder. Two men were killed near New River; Chacon got the blame. The *Tucson Citizen* editorialized that "this desperado boasted not long ago that he had killed 42 men along the border." In a front page story, the *Graham County Guardian* reported: "It is said that at least four murders stand to his credit since escaping." But there were no actual Chacon sightings. He had taken refuge in Sonora and apparently had no desire to come back to face a hangman's noose in Arizona.

Then along came the Arizona Rangers.

Captain Burt Mossman, in particular.

The Rangers were in their finals days as a crime-fighting entity. Originally organized to deter cattle rustling, they were being phased out by the state legislature as a cost-cutting measure. Under

Mossman's leadership as their first captain, the Rangers rounded up or otherwise eliminated some of the worst gangs in the territory. But Chacon had eluded him and, even though his days as a Ranger were numbered, Mossman was determined to bring him to justice. He came up with an intricate plot that involved illegal border crossings, deception, and cool heads. To help him pull it off, Mossman recruited Burt Alvord and Billy Stiles, both former lawmen who had turned outlaw and were now hiding in Mexico. Mossman offered them a deal: If they'd help capture Chacon, he'd promise them leniency if and when they came back to Arizona Territory. The two agreed, and Mossman set his plan into action.

Mossman would pose as a jail escapee who had some stolen horses for sale. Alvord and Stiles would find Chacon and offer to sell him the pilfered livestock. Chacon agreed to a meeting, but said it had to take place about twenty-five miles south of the border. Stiles brought the news back to Mossman while Alvord stayed with Chacon. Mossman hesitated. He had no authority in Mexico, and if he was caught trying to apprehend a Mexican citizen, it would create an international incident which, in the end, would work in Chacon's favor. On the other hand, four months had already passed. He decided to risk it.

Mossman and Stiles crossed the border and met the other two men at the prearranged site. It was late; they decided to make camp then head north in the morning. On the pretense of looking for firewood, Alvord saddled up and rode off. He never came back. Chacon grew antsy. He didn't trust the two remaining Americans, but his desire to acquire prime horseflesh was stronger than his anxiety.

The following morning, Mossman got the drop on Chacon and arrested him, even though it was illegal. He ordered Stiles to handcuff the desperado and tie a rope around his neck. The unlikely trio then mounted their horses and rode north, Mossman in front holding tightly to the reins of Chacon's horse and Stiles bringing up the rear while clutching the rope around the desperado's neck. They eluded border patrols and eventually arrived safely in Arizona, just as Mossman's term as a Ranger expired. The ex-Ranger alerted Graham County Sheriff Jim Parks that the trip down south had been successful. He told reporters he had captured Chacon "on a horse ranch located about seven miles this side of the Mexican line." It was a lie, but Parks would later support it. Then Mossman put Chacon into stronger handcuffs and leg irons and rode to the railroad depot at Fairbank, where Parks and his deputies waited. The lawmen and their captive returned to Solomonville by train.

During the ride back, Chacon confided that he once could have killed Parks. He said he had been hiding in a cave when Parks and his wife rode by in their buggy. Parks said he remembered. "I saw the fellow had a gun," he later told his friends, "so I handed the reins to my wife and laid my Winchester across my lap. I never realized it was Chacon until he reminded me of the incident."

Parks was a determined man who had a lengthy career in law enforcement, although it wasn't always successful. He ran for sheriff of Grant County, New Mexico, and lost. He ran for sheriff of Graham County, Arizona, and lost. During the 1885 Apache outbreaks, he became a captain in the Duncan Rangers, an Arizona militia group. He was appointed undersheriff of Graham County in 1888 and killed a man in the line of duty in 1890.

In 1892, he was named deputy sheriff in Clifton and then ran for Graham County sheriff again in 1894. He lost again, but got a job as a deputy. He was appointed a US Deputy Marshal in 1895, moved back to New Mexico and served as a deputy sheriff of Grant County, then returned to Arizona and resumed his role as a deputy at Clifton. He ran for Graham County sheriff again in 1898, and lost again. His persistence finally paid off when he won the 1900 election.

When his term expired after six years, Parks retired as a peace officer and took up ranching. He died in Clifton in 1955.

A reporter who accompanied the lawmen and Chacon wrote that the outlaw didn't look very good. "His form is bent and his head is tinged with gray," he reported. "To be hunted down like a wild animal for five years has left its mark on the outlaw . . ."

When the reporter asked where he was headed, Chacon allegedly told him, "I suppose they are taking me to Solomonville, and I want them to kill me this time. I prefer death to a term in the penitentiary."

He was about to get his wish.

The cell that awaited the outlaw wasn't the same one he'd inhabited five years earlier. The wooden flooring and adobe walls were still there, but a steel cage had been added. Authorities weren't taking any chances this time.

Justice would be swift. There was no need for a new trial because Chacon had already been convicted of murder and sentenced to hang. The gallows erected for the 1897 execution that didn't happen were still in place, hidden from view by a high adobe wall. It would not be a public event, like many other hangings had been. Only those with invitations were allowed to attend. Authorities scheduled November 14, 1902, as the new date for the hanging, then moved it to a week later when a citizens' group again petitioned to have the death penalty set aside in favor of life imprisonment. Once again, the appeal was denied.

November 21 arrived. It was a Friday. Chacon ate a hearty breakfast and visited with two friends, Sixto Molino and Jesus Bustos. He shaved off the beard he had let grow since being incarcerated, but left his trademark mustache. He asked for a priest and confessed his sins, or those acts he considered sins. Then he put on the new suit his jailers had brought him.

Shortly after noon, the guards marched him past the coffin that had been built to hold his remains, and then through a crowd of curious onlookers and protesters to the gallows. About fifty witnesses were allowed inside the adobe wall; those who weren't invited climbed nearby trees to watch the morbid happenings. When the entourage arrived at the gallows, Chacon requested one last cigarette and a cup of coffee. He finished both, and then asked if he could address the gathering. Authorities scrambled to find an interpreter because Chacon spoke very little English. When everything was set, he launched into a lengthy tirade against the legal system that had convicted him. He spoke for more than thirty minutes, admitting some crimes but fiercely denying that he was a murderer.

"I have a clean conscience," he said. "I am sure that this hand has never been guilty of murder. I may have stolen and done a good many other things, but I am innocent of this crime."

He concluded his rambling speech with: "The law never gives up and never gets out of order. If any of you intend to leave, I would like to have you all remain until the last moment, and now I would like to smoke a cigarette slowly." He asked for paper and tobacco, rolled another cigarette and smoked it while talking with the crowd and his executioner. "It is nothing but right that when one is going to die that he be given a few moments of time to quietly smoke a cigarette," he said.

When he finished, Sheriff Parks asked if he was done talking. Chacon responded, *"Si, es todo."* ("Yes, it is all.") He removed his shoes, and then stood silently as his hands were tied. His final statement: "It's too late now. It is time to hang."

His two friends climbed the steps to shake his hand. The hangman placed the noose and sprung the trap. The coroner declared him dead sixteen minutes later. The body was released to Molino and Bustos for burial. They put the corpse in a wagon and headed toward Molino's ranch.

In its report the next day, the *Arizona Bulletin* commented: "A nervier man than Augustine Chacon never walked to the gallows, and his hanging was a melodramatic spectacle that will never be forgotten by those who witnessed it."

But the execution didn't put an immediate end to the legend.

As they drove out of sight, the friends allegedly tried to revive him by forcing whiskey down his throat, rubbing his limbs to restart circulation, and covering his body with a thick blanket. When Sheriff Parks heard about it, he rushed to the ranch and ordered that Chacon's body be buried immediately. Despite that, a story circulated that the attempt had been successful, that Chacon was still alive and had returned to Mexico. Even a song was written about El Peludo. It claimed that he lived on in El Paso.

Parks put an end to such speculation when he proclaimed:

I heard reports for a while after the hanging that Chacon was being seen here and there. But I soon stopped such stories. Every time someone told me they saw Chacon, I would say that if anyone's neck could stretch that far (indicating eight inches) and still live, it was all right with me. That fellow's head did everything but come off his body.

Both Molino and Bustos denied the resurrection attempt, and when Molino's wife, Catherine, was asked about it, she replied, "I turned back the sheet and looked at him. He was dead alright. My friend Anita stayed with me all night. None of us went to bed."

Chacon was buried in the nearby San Jose Cemetery, but a dispute arose a short time later concerning the grave when a rumor spread that he had been interred in a small plot on the Molino ranch. That was soon dispelled by family members and the gravesite was officially declared as the one in the cemetery. In the 1920s, descendants dedicated a headstone at his grave. The inscription reads:

AUGUSTINE CHACON
1861 — 1902
HE LIVED LIFE WITHOUT FEAR,
HE FACED DEATH WITHOUT FEAR.
HOMBRE MUY BRAVO

CHAPTER SEVENTEEN

Billy Stiles:
Lawman Turned Outlaw Turned Lawman

In the long run, Billy Stiles fared much better as an outlaw than as a lawman. He escaped death several times while running from the law, but died while trying to enforce it.

Stiles was not all bad. He married young and worked hard as a miner, prospector, and rancher. He was an expert tracker who helped authorities apprehend the bad guys. At least twice during his short life, he served as a deputy sheriff. But, like so many others in the course of history, he fell in with evil companions and that meant trouble—the kind that led to train robbery, cattle rustling, gunfights, jail time, and jail breaks.

Much of the blame for those career choices can be traced to Albert Wright "Burt" Alvord, one of the more skilled practitioners in the art of working both sides of the law. Stiles undoubtedly would have been better off had the two never met.

William Larkin Stiles was born in Casa Grande, Arizona Territory, in 1871. His mother and her two sons had moved to the territory from Missouri after the death of her first husband, William Bible. She met and married Martin Stiles and the union produced Billy a short time later. Neither he nor his two stepbrothers got along well with the elder Stiles, who drank heavily and frequently abused the boys during his drunken rages. After one beating, Billy allegedly shot and killed his tormentor, then stole a horse and fled. He was only nine years old. During the investigation that followed, some claimed that Robert Bible, Billy's eldest stepbrother, had actually fired the fatal shot.

No one was ever charged. Billy returned home later, and then left permanently when he was about fifteen years old. Although

Billy Stiles served as both a lawman and a law breaker.
SCOTTSDALE CC SOUTHWEST STUDIES

still quite young, he found work in the mines and on ranches in the eastern part of the territory. A story circulated that he had been involved in a gunfight, but it was later exposed as a prank instigated by Stiles and some of his coworkers. Despite that, in 1895 he was hired as a deputy in a small town near Tombstone. He earned a great deal of respect when he and a companion rode one hundred miles in fourteen hours to capture a train robber. The feat impressed Wells Fargo officials, who offered him a job guarding the payrolls and other valuables carried by train. While acting in that capacity, he confronted a ticketless rider who threatened him. Fearing for his life, Stiles shot and killed the man. Shortly afterwards, he married a woman in Casa Grande.

At about that same time, Alvord was making a big name for himself in and around Tombstone. After moving to Tombstone with his father, he worked as a stable hand at the OK Corral and was a witness to the infamous shootout that took place near there. When Texas John Slaughter was elected sheriff of Cochise County in 1886, he appointed the twenty-year-old Alvord as his deputy. He served in that capacity for the next four years and became particularly adept at snooping around town to uncover information about various fugitives.

Alvord helped Slaughter track down and arrest numerous thieves and rustlers and became known as a tough lawman, feared for his deadly abilities with a six-gun. He and Slaughter usually got the men they were after, but sometimes returned from the chase without any prisoners. As his reputation as a no-nonsense lawman grew, Alvord began working the other side. After gunning down the wanted men, he confiscated valuables from their corpses but didn't turn them over to his superiors. He also pilfered a few horses and sold them across the border in Mexico. But, because he was so good as a deputy, Slaughter and the other sheriffs who employed him tended to look the other way.

In 1896, Alvord was hired as deputy constable in Pearce, a boom town near Tombstone. Gold had been discovered in the area, and the strike attracted the usual rowdies. Within weeks, the new lawman had not only turned the town into a peaceful little spot in the Sonoran Desert, but also gave every indication that he was settling down. He got married, bought a house in Pearce, and invested in a ranch in the Dragoon Mountains.

But the calm didn't last. Less than a year later, Alvord signed on as deputy constable at Willcox. A month after that, his boss resigned and Alvord moved up to the top spot. Willcox was not as easily tamed as Pearce had been. It was a rip-roaring town filled with tough cowboys who had little respect for a lawman's badge, rustlers who had no fear of the law, con artists who skirted the law, as well as bandits, thieves, brothels, and saloons. Alvord fit right in and made sure his fellow citizens knew who was boss. One episode in particular illustrated his demeanor. As a joke one night, a group of well-liquored cowboys ganged up on Alvord and locked him in the basement of a saloon, then staged a raucous party while the lawman stewed below. After the fun was over, the pranksters released their victim and one of them apologized. Alvord escorted him outside, several shots rang out and the constable returned to the bar alone. He claimed self-defense. Nobody argued.

Within a few months, Alvord was also appointed as a Cochise County deputy sheriff while retaining his post as constable of Willcox. This gave him unprecedented authority across the area, but it also meant he would have more enemies. To protect his dual positions as well as his own skin, he hired several deputies.

One of them was Billy Stiles, who quit his railroad job to become a full-time lawman.

Both of their lives would undergo drastic changes as a result.

Although they wore badges and were given prestigious titles, Alvord and Stiles realized that they'd never get rich if they adhered strictly to the activities outlined in their oaths of office. Therefore, they devised a scheme to alleviate this disparity in the distribution of wealth. It involved some illegalities, but it was so foolproof that they ignored the possibility of being caught.

They planned to hold up a Southern Pacific train carrying the payroll from the Pearce mines. The estimated take would be as much as $300,000.

It was September 9, 1899. Alvord knew the train would have to slow down to make a steep grade near Cochise, about ten miles west of Willcox. This would make it an easy target, so easy that he had little trouble convincing Stiles and two other deputies—Matt Burts and Bill Downing—to participate in the holdup. The quartet of soon-to-be robbers stole dynamite from a Willcox mercantile and blasting caps from a mining camp, then rode to the proposed site. But only Stiles and Burts stayed there. Alvord and Downing rode back into town to start the poker game that would be their alibi.

The train slowed; Stiles and Burts jumped on board. Burt held a gun on the engineer and ordered him to unhook the mail and express cars while Stiles disarmed the agents in charge of the money. They forced the trainmen to move the cars to a designated spot, then ordered them wait there while they looted the safes. One blast of dynamite did the job. The deputies-gone-bad gathered up what they could, jumped on the horses Downing and Alvord had earlier left hobbled in some brush, and brazenly rode back into Willcox.

While all that was going on, Alvord and Downing were involved in a serious poker game—or so it seemed. As part of the plan, they started playing cards in a back room at Schwertner's Saloon, and then bribed the bartender to bring them drinks and leave the room with empty glasses at regular intervals, creating the impression that the game was actually in session and that the participants were drinking rather heavily. Using the bartender as an alibi, they slipped out a side window, deposited the horses, and hastily returned to the phony game. It wasn't long before the train backed into town and news of the robbery spread like a prairie fire. Alvord sprang into action and immediately organized three posses to pursue the culprits. Stiles headed one, Burts another, and Alvord the third. All went in different directions. For obvious reasons, none of them went in the right direction. They returned at dawn without capturing anyone.

Wells Fargo detectives and the Arizona Rangers suspected Alvord. They coerced the bartender to admit his part in the scheme, but he got cold feet and vanished before charges could be filed. The plan had worked to perfection.

Flushed with their initial success, Alvord and Stiles planned another holdup. But this time, neither of them would be directly involved. Instead, they hired Bravo Juan Yoas, Three-Fingered Jack Dunlap, Bob Brown, and brothers George and Lewis Owens to do the dirty work. Stiles was assigned to track the movements of Jeff Milton, a tough Wells Fargo agent with a reputation of being fearless and a crack shot.

Milton was born in 1861, the son of Confederate Florida Governor John Milton. His father was so loyal to the Confederacy that he committed suicide when it became apparent that the South was not going to win the Civil War. Young Milton moved to Texas at age fifteen and worked as a cowboy, then lied about his age so he could join the Texas Rangers. After a four-year stint with the Rangers, he made his way to New Mexico and became a deputy US Marshal in 1884.

In one of his more memorable moments, Milton was accused of being an assassin hired by John Wesley Hardin, the notorious gunman who allegedly murdered people for no particular reason. Hardin claimed that he had paid Milton and his partner, George Scarborough, to kill a Texas rustler. Both were arrested, but then released when Hardin withdrew his accusations.

Milton later teamed up with Slaughter to help clean up in Cochise County; after that he went to work for Wells Fargo. It was during this time that he came face-to-face with the Alvord-Stiles gang.

Alvord didn't want to mess with Milton, so his orders to Stiles were direct: One way or another, make sure Milton is not on the train. Stiles went to Nogales and found out that Milton was not scheduled for that run. But at the last minute, there was a change. Milton was reassigned. Word of the switch never reached Stiles.

With Milton on board, the New Mexico & Arizona train left Nogales and headed toward Fairbank, a busy railroad hub. Stiles was making his way back to Willcox; Alvord was in Benson ordering drinks; the quintet of holdup men waited at the station. When the train stopped in Fairbank, the five bandits sprang into action. Two of them took control of the engine and the other three opened the door to the express car. Milton greeted them with a rifle and

the shooting began. One bullet tore through Milton's hat; a second severely wounded him. He grabbed a shotgun and fired a blast into Dunlap's chest. The bandits hauled their comrade off the train and fled without any money. They dumped the wounded man alongside the road where a posse found him the next day. Although mortally wounded, Dunlap survived for three days and confessed, naming Alvord as the ringleader and Stiles as one of his conspirators.

The whole gang was rounded up and held in Tombstone's jail. But Stiles was released when he agreed to become a stool pigeon. The decision to turn informer may have been made when his wife agreed to testify against him. He admitted his part in the two robberies and, like Dunlap, fingered Alvord as the brains behind them. True to form, Alvord denied everything. Less than two months later, Stiles sauntered into the jail and asked to speak with Alvord. As the jailer led him back to the cell, Stiles shoved a gun into his ribs and demanded the keys. He unlocked the cell where his associates were held and said they were free to leave. Only Alvord and Yoas accepted his offer; the others said they'd rather face trial than run. The jailer tried to stop the escapees; Stiles shot him in the leg.

All three made their way to Mexico. Yoas left for points unknown but Stiles and Alvord stayed together. As a joke, they mailed the keys back to the jail in Tombstone, along with a note saying they had witnessed a robbery but didn't arrest anyone because "we didn't have our badges." They also tried to fake their own deaths by sending two coffins with their supposed bodies inside to authorities in Tombstone. But the bodies were those of two Mexicans Stiles and Alvord had allegedly either killed during a robbery attempt or stolen from recently dug graves. When authorities unsealed the coffins and discovered that the moldering bodies inside weren't those of Alvord and Stiles, the chase was back on.

They remained on the run until Arizona Ranger Burt Mossman entered their lives. Mossman was near the end of his career with the Rangers because they were being phased out by the territorial legislature. In his final days as a Ranger, he was determined to bring desperado Augustine Chacon back from Mexico to face murder charges in Arizona. He knew Alvord and Stiles were hiding out south of the border, and he figured they could help him. He made contact and promised leniency in return for their assistance. They agreed and helped set a trap for the fearsome bandit. Alvord participated in the first part of the plan, but then fled before the actual arrest. Nevertheless, Stiles and the Ranger were successful and Chacon eventually was executed for his crimes.

Alvord crossed back into Arizona and surrendered in late 1902. Stiles was also apprehended but chose to flee rather than testify against his former boss. He was recaptured, but, rather than put him in the same lock-up as Alvord, authorities sent Stiles to Tucson and Alvord to Phoenix until their trial dates were set. When it was time for their hearing, they were returned to Tombstone and placed in the same jail. The incarceration didn't last long, however. They dug a hole in the jail's adobe wall, stole a couple of horses, and headed back to Mexico. Arizona authorities offered a $500 reward for each man while they continued their crime spree south of the border. It lasted until February 19, 1903, when the Arizona Rangers spotted the pair in Naco, Sonora, and crossed the border in pursuit. Alvord was wounded during the ensuing shootout; Stiles escaped. Alvord was arrested, charged, tried, and sentenced to a term in Yuma Territorial Prison, where he served a little more than two years. Following his release in October 1905, he moved to Los Angeles and lived with a sister, then disappeared. There were stories that he moved to Barbados, but in 1938, two of his nieces told the Arizona Historical Society that he had died on a small island off the coast of Panama around 1910. His former home in Willcox is one of the city's forty commercial and residential buildings listed on the National Register of Historic Places.

But Stiles was still loose.

Now a much-wanted man, he remained out of sight for about five years. He left the country and traveled to the Philippines and China. But he couldn't stay away from the land where he had spent most of his life, so he came back. He changed his name to

William Larkin and became a deputy sheriff in Humboldt County, Nevada. It proved to be a fatal move.

On the morning of December 5, 1908, he was gunned down while trying to serve a court summons on a ranch near Kings River, ninety miles north of Winnemucca. The summons was for Charlie Barr, a sheepherder. As Stiles, now known as Larkin, approached the camp barn, Barr stepped out from behind the building and fired three shots. All of them hit the lawman. Although mortally wounded, he managed to fire once at his assailant, but the bullet missed.

There was some initial confusion about the victim's identity. He was known as William Larkin in Nevada, but within days after his death, a woman claiming to be his sister-in-law arrived and positively identified him as Billy Stiles. Later, the woman said she was his estranged wife. There was never a reason given for the deception.

The death was reported in the *Humboldt Star* on December 7. It read, in part:

> *A dastardly murder was committed last Saturday afternoon at the Riley ranch . . . William Larkin, a deputy sheriff, being shot down in cold blood by Charley Barr, former partner of Jim Taylor, the desperado who was killed by Sheriff [S. Graham] Lamb in the performance of his duty last summer.*
>
> *The only known motive for the killing of Deputy Sheriff Larkin is revenge. Barr, according to the stories that are told, having sworn to kill those who were in any way connected with the killing of Jim Taylor. Larkin is the first victim, he having been the detective who worked up the case against Taylor last summer . . .*

The newspaper then quoted Floyd McReynolds, the ranch foreman, who witnessed the shooting. He said that after Barr fired the fatal shots, he (McReynolds) tried to run but Barr threatened to kill him if he "made an offensive move." Barr went into the ranch house and stole all the guns inside, then went to the barn, selected the best saddle horse on the ranch and turned all the other horses loose.

The story noted: "Mounting the animal, the desperado rode away in the direction of China Creek and the Oregon line but before going he warned the men on the ranch that he would kill anyone who tried to follow him to leave for town to notify the officers."

The newspaper report concluded by observing that Larkin "bore an excellent reputation, as well as being known as a fearless and capable officer. He was not a regular deputy of Sheriff Lamb, but was deputized specially for the serving of papers in a civil suit, which mission he was on at the time he was murdered."

Barr fled toward Oregon, but was captured before he got there, and ordered to stand trial. On the witness stand, Barr said he knew Stiles was after him because of a gunfight between Taylor, Barr's partner, and Sheriff Lamb as the lawman tried to make an arrest. Taylor died during the confrontation and Barr openly vowed to kill everyone involved. Larkin (Stiles), working as a detective for a group of stockmen, was involved in the investigation that led to the shootout. But at his trial, Barr pleaded self defense, claiming that Stiles had threatened him on several previous occasions. The jury apparently agreed. He was acquitted but didn't go straight. He left Nevada and moved to Colorado, where he was convicted of robbery and given a lengthy sentence.

Shortly after the trial, an area newspaper reported that Taylor's twelve-year-old son had killed Stiles with a blast from a double-barreled shotgun, but it was later proved to be only a rumor.

And a story that appeared in the *Arizona Daily Star* on November 25, 1909, either cleared up the details of his death, or created more confusion. Under the heading of "The Slayer of Billy Stiles Confesses to His Murder," it reported that there had been a mystery surrounding Stiles's death, but it had been solved when Barr confessed to the murder while being held in Cañon City, Colorado.

After noting that Larkin (Stiles) had been shot and killed from ambush in Humboldt, the story said Barr made a full confession while serving a sixteen-year sentence in the state penitentiary at Cañon City for robbing a streetcar conductor in Pueblo, Colorado. He was, according to the story, using a fake name but when authorities tied him to the murder, he admitted his guilt.

The story noted that there was some confusion since Stiles was using Larkin, his middle name, to throw other lawmen off his trail due to unserved warrants from his earlier life. But, it added, his relatives claimed to have proof that Larkin and Stiles were one and the same. The report concluded with an observation that Nevada authorities were trying to secure a pardon for Barr from Colorado so they could take him back to Nevada and prosecute him for murder.

Since Barr had already been acquitted by the Nevada jury, there is no doubt that the newspaper got many of the facts wrong. Barr was not taken back to Nevada, but there are no details about what happened to him after his time in the Colorado lock-up.

Billy Stiles, the lawman who turned outlaw before becoming a lawman again, was buried on the north bank of the Humboldt River in Winnemucca on November 9, 1908. Later, his name was added to a plaque on the Law Enforcement Memorial in Carson City, Nevada. He is also recognized as William L. Stiles at the National Peace Officers Memorial in Washington, D.C.

The location of his gravesite is uncertain. The only cemetery in Winnemucca at the time of his death was the Pioneer Cemetery on the north side of the river. But many of the graves were moved to a different cemetery on the south side of the river in the fall of 1909 due to a highway improvement project. Since records were lost during the move, nobody is sure where Stiles is buried.

Slaughter and Milton both retired from law enforcement and spent the rest of their lives in Arizona. Slaughter was a cattle rancher until his death in Douglas, Arizona, in 1922. His ranch is now a museum operated by the Arizona State Parks Department. Milton eventually recovered from his wound but never regained complete use of his arm. He settled down in Tombstone and died there in 1947.

CHAPTER EIGHTEEN

Bill Downing:
He Should Never Have Faced That Ranger

In 1959, singer Marty Robbins wrote and recorded "Big Iron," a Western ballad about a showdown between an outlaw and an Arizona Ranger. The Ranger is unnamed; his foe is Texas Red. The lawman rides into the town of Agua Fria, slowly looking up and down and carrying "a big iron on his hip." He tells the townsfolk he's there to take Texas Red, dead or alive.

Texas Red hears about the Ranger but he doesn't worry. Twenty men had already faced him; all twenty were dead and he had whittled a notch on the butt of his six-gun for each victim. As the song continues, the townspeople fear that the badge-toter is about to finish second when the two square off on the main street at 11:20 in the morning. But the Ranger wins. Texas Red never even gets his gun out of its holster before a bullet rips into his chest.

The song was originally released in September 1959 as part of an album titled *Gunfighter Ballads and Trail Songs,* then as a single six months later. Several other artists, including Johnny Cash, also recorded it; Robbins's version reached number 26 on *Billboard's* Hot 100 chart in 1960. It was even more popular than that in Willcox because that community views it as a true story.

Or partially true.

Robbins visited the city frequently because he was a friend of Willcox native Rex Allen, who left his hometown to become famous as a Western singer, movie star, television hero, and the voice of several Walt Disney cartoon characters. Allen appeared as one of the last singing cowboys during the heyday of the B-Western movie era, then moved on to become the star of *Frontier Doc-*

Jackson, - alias
Bill Downing.

Bill Downing met his fate at the hands of an Arizona Ranger.
COURTESY OF THE ARIZONA HISTORICAL SOCIETY, TUCSON (4924)

tor, a television series. He and Robbins occasionally performed together in the local theater, and Robbins became familiar with the history of the area. One incident particularly fascinated him. It was true, and it dealt with the shootout that became the basis for "Big Iron."

The actual version didn't happen quite the way it did in the song, but there are enough similarities to support the contention that Robbins based his lyrics on the event. At least, that's how they tell it in Willcox.

In the real story, the principal characters weren't an anonymous Ranger and Texas Red; they were William Slaughter "Billy" Speed, an Arizona Ranger, and W. F. "Bill" Downing, an outlaw who had been involved in a long list of illegal activities, including murder, prostitution, and a series of train robberies. And Speed carried a rifle, not a six-gun. But, although the circumstances were different, the outcome was the same.

Downing was not very popular, regardless of where he lived. He was vile-tempered and had such a bad reputation that most people referred to him as "Quarrelsome Bill." He came to Willcox around 1883 and hired on as a hand at the Esperanza Ranch in the Dragoon Mountains; his coworkers soon discovered that he had a bad attitude, particularly when he'd been drinking. When that job didn't work out, he and his wife moved to nearby Willcox. A short time later, Downing allied himself with Albert "Burt" Alvord, the town constable. That association would set the pattern for the remainder of his life because Alvord was hardly a paragon of virtue, despite his status as a lawman.

Downing's first recorded brush with the law occurred one night in 1899, when he tangled with William "Slim" Traynor in a local saloon. Traynor was another tough frontiersman who, in the words of his contemporaries, "wasn't afraid of anything." He had been an outlaw and a mine guard and had served as a Rough Rider in the First US Cavalry. In 1898, he was hired to oversee a ranch operation near Willcox. He and Downing became friends and stayed that way until Traynor began suspecting that Downing was "brand burning," a common term usually associated with changing the brands on rustled cattle. Although Traynor openly voiced his suspicions, he made no direct threats toward Downing. But Quarrelsome Bill didn't take the accusations so lightly, especially when he was drinking. Many times, the locals said, he "made some kind of threats about what he was going to do," and what he was going to do usually involved a pointed six-gun.

Despite all that, the two were cordial toward each other when they met in the Elite Saloon on the evening of May 19, 1899. Downing was already seated and having a drink when Traynor walked in and took up a spot at the bar. His companion, Henry Taylor, stood next to him, and then turned away from the bar to check out the crowd. He didn't see Downing at first, but spotted Tom Burts and offered to buy him a shot of whiskey. As Burts rose to accept, Downing also got up and began walking toward the bar, so Taylor included him in the gesture. As he approached, Traynor turned to face him. Burts later described what happened next:

"I had not reached the bar at that time but was standing to the left of Traynor and partly behind him. Downing grabbed me by the left arm and jerked me around and back nearly facing him and said something which I did not understand. Downing then fired. I thought when he fired the first shot that he was firing at me and also thought so when he fired the second shot. I think there was four shots fired. During the shooting, the room was full of smoke and the firing very close and just in front of me, and I did not know who he was firing at unless at me."

But Downing wasn't firing at Burts. He was aiming at Traynor. Three of his four shots hit his intended target, one in the chest and two in the head.

Downing was arrested and put on trial. He claimed self-defense. He said he thought Traynor was going for his gun, and "on account of the threats he had made . . . I thought it was a life-and-death matter and drew my gun and jerked Thomas Burts back so as not to shoot him and commenced shooting." He said he didn't remember how many shots he fired.

Alvord, in his role as constable, testified that when he examined the body, he found the dead man's pistol still in its holster. But the coroner's jury agreed with Downing that the shooting was in self defense and therefore justified. He was acquitted.

Within months, Downing's association with Alvord began to reap temporary rewards. They joined forces with Matt Burts and Billy Stiles, one of Alvord's deputies, and planned a train robbery. It was a near-perfect operation. While Alvord and Downing played poker in the back room of a Willcox saloon to establish an alibi, the other two held up the train at Cochise Station, about eleven miles west of town. They got away with more than $2,000, and then raced back into town to report the robbery. Alvord organized a posse that included the three outlaws and they hustled out of town. But, for obvious reasons, nobody was ever captured.

The venture wasn't a complete success, however. At least, not for Downing. He was later indicted for his participation in the holdup and went to trial in December 1900. But he got off due to a disagreement over a technicality. The train robbery was a capital offense that demanded a death sentence, but almost two hundred potential jurors were excused because they thought the penalty was worse than the crime. A report in the *Arizona Daily Citizen* noted: "While many believed in capital punishment, they would not apply such a penalty in cases where no lives were lost." When a panel of jurors finally was selected, the presiding judge warned them that if they found Downing guilty, he would be forced to impose the death sentence.

After a lengthy deliberation, the jury returned a verdict of not guilty, and the *Bisbee Daily Review* summed it up: "The fact is that members of the jury were firmly convinced that the defendant was guilty of train robbery, but notwithstanding the Arizona statute making the offense punishable by death, they refused to return a verdict of guilty."

But Downing wasn't free to go home and continue his wanton ways. Three months later, he was indicted on a federal charge of attempting to rob the United States Mail and assaulting a mail clerk. This time, the jury found him guilty after a five-day trial and ordered a ten-year sentence in the Arizona Territorial Prison at Yuma. He entered prison on April 11, 1901, wearing inmate number 1733. Little more than a year later, his wife died in Tucson, where she had moved after the trial and found work as a domestic. A coroner's inquest ruled that she had died of heart failure, probably brought on by her husband's conviction. Downing unexpectedly became such a model prisoner that he got time off for good behavior and served less than six years.

His nice demeanor, or whatever it was that got the sentence reduced, didn't last. Downing returned to Willcox and opened the Free and Easy Saloon, a bar that offered both liquor and women and didn't ask questions. His disposition varied between barely tolerable to downright mean. That was nothing out of the ordinary in Willcox, however, because the town was a known hangout for rustlers, gamblers, and a wide variety of outlaws. An area newspaper termed it a place where "nothing from gambling to shooting up the town was barred."

Downing's encounters with the law became standard topics of conversation. He was accused of being perpetually drunk and disorderly. He was busted for allowing acts of prostitution on his property and paid a $50 fine. He was charged with assault and fined $10. Eventually, the other businessmen got fed up with his lawbreaking antics and began circulating a petition to have his saloon license revoked. When Downing retaliated with threats, they appealed to the Arizona Rangers to help get rid of him. Ranger Captain Harry Wheeler had already received word that Downing had vowed to kill any lawman who messed with him. Billy Speed, the resident Ranger, was out of town at the time, so Wheeler sent two of his men who were stationed along the border at Naco to investigate. And he ordered them to shoot Downing if he gave them any trouble. When they arrived, however, they found the saloon keeper in such a pleasant mood that they left town without taking any action.

But Wheeler was wary. He wrote to Speed and warned him that Downing, as a "known defier of the law," should be kept under constant watch. He also informed Speed that Downing had threatened to "blow the head off of any lawman" who interfered with his business, then issued a written order to take drastic action if the need arose. Wheeler wrote:

> *I hereby direct you to prepare yourself to meet this man whenever a warrant is placed in your hands for his arrest, and upon his least or slightest attempt to do you harm, I want you to kill him, for I believe he will otherwise kill you. He is determined to kill someone, and it is a certainty that he desires to murder several people in Willcox . . . I want you to take no chance with this man in any official dealing you may have with him. Of course, I would desire a peaceful arrest, but if anyone must be hurt, it must not be you.*

Speed tucked the letter into a shirt pocket but heeded its contents. Downing had already been suspected in as many as thirty deaths. And he and Downing had tangled before, once when Speed had served on the coroner's jury that heard the evidence in the death of Slim Traynor; later when the Ranger appeared as a witness for the prosecution during Downing's trial for train robbery. As a result, Downing's bitterness toward lawmen in general and Speed in particular turned to abject hatred. He boasted that if Speed even stuck his head into his saloon, he'd shoot it off. And, he added, "If he does not come in, I will kill the son of a bitch anyway, when the time comes."

In early August 1908, Downing got into a major disagreement with Cuco Leal, who lived in the back of his saloon. Downing wanted her to leave; she didn't want to go. Since he hated Speed, Downing contacted Bud Snow, the town constable, to handle the matter and the lawman brokered an uneasy peace treaty. That didn't last long. The two combatants went at it again the next night when Downing accused the woman of stealing money from him and she whacked him with a whiskey glass. Now fearing for her life, Leal fled from the Free and Easy Saloon and was given shelter in a rival bar owned by George McKittrick, another Downing enemy. McKittrick swore out a warrant for Downing's arrest and the judge in charge handed it over to the constable, who immediately contacted Speed. The Ranger said he'd take care of it the next morning.

Downing was already drunk when the next morning arrived. He was in an ugly mood, and complained to Ralph Cushman, a drinking companion, that "they are after me." Word of the warrant for his arrest had arrived at his place of business so he armed himself and told Cushman he was going to the judge's office to settle the issue. But Cushman warned him that carrying a gun under those circumstances would be a big mistake. He advised Downing to "act like a man and go down and pay your fine if you are guilty, and if you are not guilty, you could get clear." Downing staggered behind the bar and retrieved the pistol he kept there. Cushman immediately said, "Don't be a damned fool," and told him to leave the gun behind. In a rare departure from form, Downing listened to the advice. He put the gun down on the bar, walked through the front door of his establishment, and headed down the street just as the sun began its daily ascent above the eastern horizon.

It was Wednesday, August 5, 1908.

Speed was getting a shave when Constable Snow brought word that Downing had left his saloon. Armed with the warrant and a Winchester rifle, the Ranger removed the barber's towel and walked outside alongside Snow. Both were fully aware that there was more than likely going to be trouble. Downing saw them and ducked into a nearby building. But the barber spotted him and yelled a warning to the lawman. Snow ran into an alley while Downing left his hiding place and walked toward Speed.

The confrontation lasted only a few moments. At first, Downing complied when Speed told him to raise his hands. But then he lowered them and appeared to reach for the pistol he usually carried. It was a fatal move. He apparently had forgotten that his gun was still back in the saloon. Speed reacted instantly and fired one shot from his rifle. And, just as in the song, the Ranger's aim was deadly. The slug tore into Downing's chest. He died on the spot.

And nobody felt bad about it.

A coroner's jury quickly assembled and ruled that "the shot was fired by said Speed in the performance of his duty as an officer and that he was perfectly justified in the act and, therefore, we exonerate him from all blame in the matter."

Speed's supervisor, Ranger Captain Wheeler, commented, "This is the first time I have known a dead man to be without a single friend and the first time that I have known a killing to meet with absolute general rejoicing . . ."

A later report by an anonymous Ranger stated: "Bill Downing was one of the most universally disliked desperadoes in southern Arizona. He bullied men and beat up women. Even his fellow outlaws couldn't stand him . . ."

But Jack White, the sheriff of Cochise County, offered a sort of left-handed defense for the man. He said that Downing had looked well after his release from prison, but not long afterward, he became worried and despondent, and spent most of his time drinking. White said he believed that Downing was sick of living and deliberately walked to his death at the hands of the Ranger.

Within days of the showdown, Willcox residents drew up a petition requesting that the Cochise County board of supervisors withdraw the liquor license for the Free and Easy Saloon and never grant another one. Almost everyone asked to sign the document did so.

Willcox has settled down quite nicely. Now a city of about 3,800, it still takes pride in its Western heritage and for the town's forty residential and commercial buildings listed on the National Register of Historic Places.

Marty Robbins held a place of honor in the community for a brief period, with the Marty Robbins Museum just down the street from the Allen memorials. It was not a successful venture, however.

Nevertheless, Rex Allen remains a local hero even more than a decade after his death. He grew up there, and is fondly remembered as "the cross-eyed country singer who made it big" as a

B-Western movie star and national recording star. He stayed close to his roots, returning to Willcox every year for Rex Allen Days, and then moving back for good when he retired from show business. After his death in 1999, his ashes were scattered around the life-size bronze sculpture of him that stands in a downtown park, directly across the street from the Rex Allen Arizona Cowboy Museum and Willcox Cowboy Hall of Fame.

Bibliography

JACOB WALTZ

Black, Harry G. *The Lost Dutchman Mine.* Brandon Press, 1975.

Kollenborn, Tom. *The Lost Dutchman's Mine: History and Bibliography.* Apache Junction Library. 1998.

Lowe, Sam. "Arizona's Lost Treasures: They're Still Waiting." *Mysteries and Legends of Arizona.* Globe Pequot Press, 2009.

Storm, Barry. *Thunder God's Gold.* Southwest Publishing Company, 1945.

JOHNNY RINGO

Burrows, Jack. *John Ringo: The Gunfighter Who Never Was.* University of Arizona Press, 1987, 1996.

Christensen, Christina. "Johnny Ringo: The Gentleman Outlaw." www.angelfire.com/co4/earpgang/ringo02.html.

McNeer, Harry and Ingrid. "Johnny Ringo Grave Site." www.ghost towns.com/states/az.

"Outlaw Found Dead." *Arizona Daily Star,* July 18, 1882.

Parsons, George. Diary excerpt. March 22, 1882.

Trimble, Marshall. "Johnny Ringo: Outlaw." *In Old Arizona.* Gold West Publishers, 1985.

CURLY BILL BROCIUS

"Marshall Shot!" *Tombstone Daily Epitaph,* October 28, 1880.

Gatto, Steve. "Tombstone Archive and Research Center." http://tombstonehistory.tripod.com/archive.html. June 2000.

The High Chaparral website. www.thehighchaparral.com.

Osborn, Jim. "Tombstone Gang Leader." www.suite101.com. February 15, 2009.

IKE CLANTON

Ayoob, Massad. "The Killing of Ike Clanton." *American Handgunner,* May-June 2009.

Aros, Joyce. "Who Were These Men? Ike Clanton." *Tombstone Times,* March 2008.

"Detailed Statements of the Killing of Ike Clanton by Detective Brighton." *Apache County Critic,* June 18, 1887.

Tombstone Daily Epitaph, June 9, 1881.

JOE BOOT

Anderson, Parker. *How a Woman Stagecoach Robber Became a Famous Outlaw.* Sharlot Hall Museum Days Past Archives, July 26, 2002.

Lowe, Sam. "Pearl Hart: The Last Stagecoach Robber." *Mysteries and Legends of Arizona.* Globe Pequot Press, 2009.

Murphy, Marti. *The Prison Chronicle: Yuma Territorial Prison's Colorful Past.* Arizona State Parks Board, 1999.

THE GOOFY, THE BAD, AND THE UNSUCCESSFUL

Anderson, Dorothy. *Arizona Legends and Lore.* Golden West Publishers, 2005.

Banks, Leo. "On-trial Cattle Rustler 'Alters' the Evidence." *Arizona Highways,* July 2003.

Bigando, Robert. *Globe, Arizona: The Life and Times of a Western Mining Town.* Mountain Spirit Press, 1989.

Haak, W. A. *Copper Bottom Tales.* Globe Historical Society, 1991.

Hatch, JoAnn. *Lore and Legend.* Kymera Publishing, 2007.

Ruffner, Melissa. *Prescott: A Pictorial History.* Primrose Press, 1981.

Snow, Glenn. *Fool's Gold: The Mining Schemes of Anthony Blum.* Research paper for Gleeson Jail Museum, 2010.

Trimble, Marshall. "Inept Bandits Have a Blast." *Arizona Highways,* July 2003.

Richard C. Flower

Donaldson, W. Scott. *Arizona Mining Scams and Unassayable Ore Projects of the Late 20th Century.* Report prepared for Arizona Mines and Mineral Resources, December 2001.

Herbert, Harold. "George Smalley, Territorial Journalism and the Spenazuma Mining Fraud." *Journal of Arizona History,* Summer 2005.

Ridgeway, Ryder. *Spenazuma.* Mt. Graham Profiles. Graham County Historical Society, 1990.

Trimble, Marshall. "Doc Flowers, Arizona Con Man." *In Old Arizona.* Gold West Publishers, 1985.

Charles Stanton

Anderson, Parker. *The 1886 Martin Family Massacre.* Sharlot Hall Museum Days Past, August 20, 2006.

Brillhart, Larry. *Rich History Makes Stanton a Popular Rendezvous.* Gold Prospectors Association Outings, May 5, 2010.

Stanton, Charles P. "Stanton in His Own Words." *Arizona Miner,* June 18, 1879. (Edited by Parker Anderson in 2005 for Sharlot Hall Museum Days Past.)

Varney, Philip. "Location of Stanton Ghost Town." *Arizona Ghost Towns and Mining Camp.* Arizona Highways, 2000.

Zlatevski, Bobby. "Stanton." www.ghosttowns.com/statesd/az. 2008.

Sofia Treadway Reavis

Lowe, Sam. "The Man Who Conned Arizona." *Mysteries and Legends of Arizona.* Globe Pequot Press, 2009.

Myers, John. "The Prince of Swindlers." *American Heritage Magazine,* May 1956.

"Saloons and Badmen." Arizona Genealogy Trails website. http://genealogytrails.com/ariz/badmen.html.

Ernesto Miranda

Arizona State Library, Archives and Public Records, 176 #107, Maricopa County.

AZ v. Ernesto Miranda.

Miranda v. Arizona, II, Title III. Series.

Sonneborn, Liz. *Supreme Court Cases Through Primary Sources.* Rosen Publishing Group, 2004.

Stuart, Gary. *The Story of America's Right to Remain Silent.* University of Arizona Press, 2006.

Randy Greenawalt

Bronson, Peter. "A Lethal Injection of Injustice." *Cincinnati Enquirer,* February 2, 1997.

Bui, Lynh. "Marking 100 Years of Incarceration." *Arizona Republic,* July 12, 2008.

Kramer, Brian. "Prison Break." *Casa Grande Dispatch,* September 9, 2011.

Rawlinson, John. "Father Ran at Shootout, They Report." *Arizona Daily Star,* April 11, 1978.

Suprynowicz, Vin. "Finally, the Murderer of Theresa Tyson May Die." *Libertarian Enterprise,* February 2, 1997.

Shady Ladies

"CRIME: Cheerful Eva." *Time,* March 3, 1930.

Lowe, Sam. "Gabrielle Darley: Heartless Murderer or Innocent Victim." *Mysteries and Legends of Arizona*. Globe Pequot Press, 2009.

United Press International. "Death Penalty Paid by Mrs. Eva Dugan." March 3, 1930.

Van Ostrand, Maggie. "Katie Elder: Her True Story." www.texas escapes.com. 2009.

Weiser, Kathy. *Big Nose Kate*. Legends of America, 2008.

JOHN SHAW

Bell, Bob Boze. "Devil Canyon Shootout." *True West,* August 1, 2008.

Gray-Searles, Tammy. "Saloon Robber Treated to One Last Drink After Death." *Horizon: Northeastern Arizona Travel Guide,* 2010.

Richardson, Cecil Calvin. "Canyon Diablo: The Roughest, Toughest Hellhole of Them All." *Arizona Highways,* April 1991.

Richardson, Gladwell. "A Drink for the Dead." *Arizona Highways,* June 1963.

Thomas, Bob. "Shootout in Canyon Diablo." *Arizona Highways,* April 1999.

"Wigwam Held Up." *Winslow Mail,* April 8, 1905.

GIOVANNI VIGLIOTTO

Arizona Department of Corrections. www.azcorrections.gov/inmate_datasearch/Index_Minh.aspx.

Associated Press. *New York Times.* "Man with 105 Wives Is Sentenced to 34 Years." March 29, 1983.

Fitzpatrick, Tom. "The Lover." *Phoenix New Times,* February 6, 1991.

Giovanni Vigliotto v. Frank Terry. US Court of Appeals.

Hemphill, Russ. "Hemorrhage Proves Fatal to Vigliotto." *Phoenix Gazette,* February 1, 1991.

"He Won 105 Hands, Loses Trial," *Time,* February 21, 1983.

Newhaus, Cable. "Scorned and Swindled by Her Bigamist Husband, Sharon Vigliotto Got Mad, Then Got Even." *People,* April 12, 1982.

"Too Much Sex Kills Man With 105 Wives!" *Weekly World News,* March 12, 1991.

Andy Cooper Blevins

"Arizona Legends: Pleasant Valley War." Arizona Genealogy Trails website. http://genealogytrails.com/ariz/pleasantwar.html.

"Arizona Legends: Pleasant Valley War." Legends of America website. www.legendsofamerica.com/az-pleasantvalleywar.html.

Barger, Matthew. *Holbrook, Arizona Guide.* Holbrook Chamber of Commerce, 2002.

Branning, Debe. "Ghostly Shootout on Joy Nevin Avenue." www.examiner.com. April 5, 2010.

Lewis, Vince. "Commodore Perry Owens." http://vincelewis.net/owens.html.

Trimble, Marshall. "Pleasant Valley War." *In Old Arizona.* Gold West Publishers, 1985.

Augustine Chacon

Brown, Nancy. Find a Grave Memorial. www.findagrave.com/cgi-bin/fg.cgi?page=gr&Grid=24403261. February 4, 2008.

Cleere, Jan. "Augustine Chacon: Hombre Muy Malo." *Outlaw Tales of Arizona.* TwoDot, 2006.

Ridgeway, Ryder. *Hombre Muy Bravo.* Mt. Graham Profiles. Graham County Historical Society, 1990.

Trimble, Marshall. "Chacon, Last of the Desperados." *In Old Arizona.* Gold West Publishers, 1985.

Billy Stiles

Dayhuff, Robert, and James Pearson. *Notorious Arizona Characters.* Santa Cruz Valley Press, 2006.

Hickson, Howard. "Billy Stiles, Lawman/Outlaw." *Howard Hickson's Histories,* February 3, 2003. www2.gbcnv.edu/howh.

Kathy Weiser. "Lawman Turned Outlaw." *Legends of America,* updated June 2010.

"William Larkin Stiles." *The Humboldt Star,* December 7, 1908. www.hoffmemorial.org/enshrined-officers/william-larkin-stiles.

Bill Downing:

Cleere, Jan. "Albert Wright 'Burt' Alvord." *Outlaw Tales of Arizona.* TwoDot, 2006.

Lowe, Sam. "Tales of Willcox." *Arizona Republic,* June 28, 2007.

Tanner, Karen, and John D. "The Lowdown on Quarrelsome Bill Downing." *Wild West*, January 30, 2009.

Index

It was September 9, 1899. Alvord knew the train would have to slow down to make a steep grade near Cochise, about ten miles west of Willcox. This would make it an easy target, so easy that he had little trouble convincing Stiles and two other deputies—Matt Burts and Bill Downing—to participate in the holdup. The quartet of soon-to-be robbers stole dynamite from a Willcox mercantile and blasting caps from a mining camp, then rode to the proposed site. But only Stiles and Burts stayed there. Alvord and Downing rode back into town to start the poker game that would be their alibi.

The train slowed; Stiles and Burts jumped on board. Burt held a gun on the engineer and ordered him to unhook the mail and express cars while Stiles disarmed the agents in charge of the money. They forced the trainmen to move the cars to a designated spot, then ordered them wait there while they looted the safes. One blast of dynamite did the job. The deputies-gone-bad gathered up what they could, jumped on the horses Downing and Alvord had earlier left hobbled in some brush, and brazenly rode back into Willcox.

While all that was going on, Alvord and Downing were involved in a serious poker game—or so it seemed. As part of the plan, they started playing cards in a back room at Schwertner's Saloon, and then bribed the bartender to bring them drinks and leave the room with empty glasses at regular intervals, creating the impression that the game was actually in session and that the participants were drinking rather heavily. Using the bartender as an alibi, they slipped out a side window, deposited the horses, and hastily returned to the phony game. It wasn't long before the train backed into town and news of the robbery spread like a prairie fire. Alvord sprang into action and immediately organized three posses to pursue the culprits. Stiles headed one, Burts another, and Alvord the third. All went in different directions. For obvious reasons, none of them went in the right direction. They returned at dawn without capturing anyone.

Wells Fargo detectives and the Arizona Rangers suspected Alvord. They coerced the bartender to admit his part in the scheme, but he got cold feet and vanished before charges could be filed. The plan had worked to perfection.

Flushed with their initial success, Alvord and Stiles planned another holdup. But this time, neither of them would be directly involved. Instead, they hired Bravo Juan Yoas, Three-Fingered Jack Dunlap, Bob Brown, and brothers George and Lewis Owens to do the dirty work. Stiles was assigned to track the movements of Jeff Milton, a tough Wells Fargo agent with a reputation of being fearless and a crack shot.

Milton was born in 1861, the son of Confederate Florida Governor John Milton. His father was so loyal to the Confederacy that he committed suicide when it became apparent that the South was not going to win the Civil War. Young Milton moved to Texas at age fifteen and worked as a cowboy, then lied about his age so he could join the Texas Rangers. After a four-year stint with the Rangers, he made his way to New Mexico and became a deputy US Marshal in 1884.

In one of his more memorable moments, Milton was accused of being an assassin hired by John Wesley Hardin, the notorious gunman who allegedly murdered people for no particular reason. Hardin claimed that he had paid Milton and his partner, George Scarborough, to kill a Texas rustler. Both were arrested, but then released when Hardin withdrew his accusations.

Milton later teamed up with Slaughter to help clean up in Cochise County; after that he went to work for Wells Fargo. It was during this time that he came face-to-face with the Alvord-Stiles gang.

Alvord didn't want to mess with Milton, so his orders to Stiles were direct: One way or another, make sure Milton is not on the train. Stiles went to Nogales and found out that Milton was not scheduled for that run. But at the last minute, there was a change. Milton was reassigned. Word of the switch never reached Stiles.

With Milton on board, the New Mexico & Arizona train left Nogales and headed toward Fairbank, a busy railroad hub. Stiles was making his way back to Willcox; Alvord was in Benson ordering drinks; the quintet of holdup men waited at the station. When the train stopped in Fairbank, the five bandits sprang into action. Two of them took control of the engine and the other three opened the door to the express car. Milton greeted them with a rifle and